Gordon Wells

The Craft
of
Writing Articles

A practical guide

Allison & Busby
London

First published in Great Britain 1983 by Allison & Busby Limited
6a Noel Street, London W1V 3RB.

British Library Cataloguing in Publication Data
Wells, Gordon
The craft of writing articles.
1. Authorship
I. Title
808'.02   PN145
ISBN 0-85031-507-7

Set in 10/11pt Times by Top Type Phototypesetting Co. Ltd., London W1.
Printed and bound in Finland by Werner Söderström Oy.

The Craft of Writing Articles

Contents

1

Introduction

So you'd like to write for magazines and newspapers? Good. It's a great occupation. If you will work at it you will surely succeed. There is always room for another new writer.

You will sell your work to editors: your words and thoughts will be read with interest by thousands of people. Your literary efforts may — perhaps — be less artistic than your friends' pottery or paintings, but they will be far more widely appreciated. The achievement of publication is every bit as welcome as the satisfaction gained from any other creative craft. And you will know that your work is good enough to sell in an open, competitive, market.

And anyone can do it. You don't need to be a literary genius — that could indeed be a disadvantage. You don't even need to have done well at English in school. Editors are more interested in good ideas than beautiful phrases. (And editors, just as writers, are as likely to be women as men, but for convenience I have referred to them throughout in the third person as "he".)

The surest way of getting into print in a magazine or newspaper is to write feature material; not the short stories or poems favoured by some as "more creative", but hard factual articles. The demand — the market — for articles is far greater than that for short stories. Taking a random sample of magazines from my shelves and counting only the obvious outside contributions, there are at least four times as many articles as stories. (The sixteen publications that I looked at comprised seven women's magazines, six general interest magazines, and just three "technical" magazines. If all published journals were to be considered — with the preponderance of specialist magazines that there is — the ratio of articles to stories would be even greater.)

And poetry has very little chance of achieving paid magazine publication at all.

A paying hobby

To emphasize the point already touched on above, one of the benefits of article-writing is that it is a paying hobby. The cash outlay is small; the rewards can be large. The annual *Writers' and Artists' Yearbook* lists over six hundred magazines published in Britain that accept and pay for factual articles. Most of these magazines rely on freelance contributors offering them material on spec: if the supply were to dry up, these magazines could not continue for long. And the yearbook is not a complete list of all magazines open to the freelance writer; many small or limited-interest magazines, which are often very good markets, are left out.

It is not easy to quantify the financial side of article-writing. It is, after all, a market-place in which we are operating. Editors may pay more for a particularly interesting article than for a more run-of-the-mill one. Payment, too, will often depend on the editor's assessment of the author's fame (if any). A magazine with a large circulation will usually pay more than one with a small circulation. But a glossy prestigious magazine will often pay less than a more popular "down-market" paper. And usually, of course, a longer article earns more than a short one.

There are British magazines that pay hundreds of pounds for an article of perhaps two thousand words. There are others that pay no more than a few pounds. Freelance writers supply material at both extremes of payment. The great majority of articles are at present paid for at between £15 and £50 per thousand words. One of my favourite markets consistently pays me £25 for articles of 600-650 words. Another pays a flat £15 for each thousand-word article — and expects illustrations to be included within that price.

Writing in English means that magazines elsewhere in the world are also open to the British freelance writer. American magazines, particularly, often pay very high rates for material suited to their specific needs. But overseas markets require special study and should not be attempted until a writer is already successful on his/her home market ground.

Whatever the rate of payment though, the principle is the same. My work — and yours too, if you are prepared to work at it until you are successful — is worth buying. Each editor's acceptance is a "prize" in the ongoing writing competition.

The purpose of this book is to explain the craft of article-writing as an enjoyable and paying hobby. It is of course possible to make freelance article-writing a full-time occupation — but this is not a practical proposition for most people. It is *not* what this book is about. I write — very profitably — in my spare time: this book is based on my years of such experience. I would not presume to advise on full-time writing practices which are outside my experience.

I make money from writing articles in my spare time — and I have fun doing so. So, too, can you.

What it takes

Having determined that you want to write; that the openings for articles are better than for other forms of writing; and that you can make money at writing; let us look at what it takes to be an article-writer.

Three qualities particularly are needed to make a success of article-writing:

- some ability to write,
- an enquiring mind (and usefully, but not essentially, a seeing eye),
- a professional approach.

Writing ability

If you can write a "newsy" letter or advise your neighbour how to prune his or her roses, you can write an article. It doesn't matter a bit that you were never good at writing "compositions" or essays at school. Article-writing is not a particularly *literary* exercise. Clarity is far more important than "Quality".

Having said that, it is nevertheless essential that you enjoy — or can grow to enjoy — stringing words together. And one of the best ways of learning to string words together is to see how others do it — by reading. Read widely, and catholically.

Read the English classic novels and read — particularly — the daily tabloids. Read the articles that others write about "your" subjects, and read "pulp" novels. And always, as you read, study how the words are put together. Notice how the tabloids favour short, easy to read, sentences: note the beauty — and sometimes the "heaviness" — of many classics and the soporific effect of learned articles.

Note, particularly, the lengths of sentences and paragraphs, and the complexity of the words. In Chapter 5, where we look at the actual writing process, I advise you to keep sentences and paragraphs short and words simple. This is fundamental.

No one can really teach you how to write though. In this book I offer guidance on what works for me. An "on the spot" teacher might perhaps correct faults, but only you can write your own words in your own way. But however you write, if you hope to sell, write so that it is easy to read: think of the reader. Abandon any literary pretensions and put aside all delusions of literary grandeur. Your aim, as an article-writer in search of paid publication, must be to write interestingly — not impressively. And simplicity and clarity come from using short words and short sentences.

The enquiring mind

The ability to write in a way that will interest readers springs from what can best be called an "enquiring mind". Just as a young child absorbs information by asking seemingly incessant questions, so too does an article-writer develop interesting subjects.

The article-writer reads a tiny snippet of news or information and ponders on it. Why did this happen? Is this the first time? What was the cause of it? Who did it first? What will come next? Where did that come from? How was it made? Can it be done again? Chapter 2 considers how article ideas can develop from such pondering.

The ordinary reader reads, and having read, moves on. The article-writer stops. Automatically, he wonders whether he can write an article about anything that interests him — and he is interested in almost everything. This is one of the side benefits of article-writing as a hobby; it broadens your interests; it can make you a more interesting person. When the article-writer is interested in a subject he will write interestingly about it — and interesting articles are saleable articles.

As already remarked, editors are not particularly concerned about writing style — their needs are simpler. They want articles to be interesting, original and easy to read. Accuracy is taken for granted — if you are found to be inaccurate it will be a long time before you sell the next article — and humour is a rare bonus.

An article on a topical subject will almost always be of interest. A successful article-writer will often be able to provide a topical tag for an otherwise straight forward general-interest factual article. Such tags are of most importance when submitting articles to daily newspapers.

The professional approach

We have just noted that editors expect the work being offered to them to be easy to read. This perhaps exemplifies the professional approach to article-writing. If your work is to sell it must be written with that object always in mind. Think of who is to read what you write. You are writing for the "average reader". Don't write to please yourself; write to attract and interest the magazine-rack-browser. If you write for yourself you could find yourself the only reader — and that is both pointless and profitless.

The successful article-writer assesses the likely reader of his work. Then he writes in a way that that reader will find easy to read. Chapter 3 explains how to assess the typical reader of a magazine and Chapter 4 discusses how to use a typical article as a "model".

But there is more to producing a saleable article than the mere writing. Indeed the actual stringing together of the words is little more than twenty per cent of the craft of article-writing. If you are to write with the object of selling your work — and thereby having it read by thousands of people throughout the land — you must undertake a more comprehensive routine.

From start to finish the article-writing process entails:

- getting an idea for an article (or better, for a set of articles) — which represents about twenty per cent of the process;
- investigating the subject, collecting material, etc. — about thirty per cent of the whole process;
- determining suitable markets for the article(s) — an essential twenty per cent of the process;
- writing up the material — amounting to little more than about twenty per cent of the job;
- preparing and presenting the article to the editor, and keeping records and accounts — the final ten per cent.

The first three components listed above — the idea, the subject research and the market research — are closely interlinked. Often an idea will come first. But an idea is not enough on its own, it has to be an idea suitable for a specific market. And unless there is enough material available to produce an article, an idea is of little use. Sometimes ideas spring directly from market research. Similarly, subject research is often the ongoing process from which many ideas spring.

It is best to think of the idea, the subject research and the market research as three inseparable and inter-related parts of the process. All three components are essential prerequisites of the writing and presentation processes. In all, they account for some seventy per cent of the article-writer's activities.

Adopting a professional approach to article-writing also entails being business-like. Any good businessman seeks to maximize his productivity and minimize his outlay; applying these principles to article-writing we must look carefully at the three components discussed above.

If you can sell several different articles on the same general subject you can reduce the effort on subject research. One outlay of research time means that only the remaining seventy per cent of effort is needed for subsequent articles. As an example, I have written several times, for different markets, about unusual hats. Latterly, I need do no more than merely up-date my basic subject research.

Similarly, writing a series of articles for a single magazine does not entail repeated market research; an awareness of any significant changes in the magazine's general approach is all that is needed. Writing a regular column for a magazine is a way of economizing on at least twenty per cent of the effort — for the selling too is already done.

The actual writing of each article is something that cannot be reduced. Indeed, anyone who enjoys their work would not wish to avoid the task of choosing the words, stringing them together and then the polishing of the final result. In Chapter 5, while unable to lay down hard and fast rules about the very personal craft of writing, there are useful guidelines — rules of thumb — for simple, easy-to-read writing.

And the final, ten per cent, part of the professional approach to article-writing is the preparation and presentation of your work to the editor. You are seeking to sell your wares. So present your work in the form that editors require. Basically, this means that it must be typed, double-spaced, on one side only of A4 paper. If you don't present your work in this way it just will not usually be considered. There is no way you can buck the system. Further details of the presentation of your work are contained in Chapter 7.

The seeing eye

There is one further aspect of the article-writing craft which has to be mentioned. Some subjects lend themselves to, or positively call for, being illustrated. Freelance article-writers who can provide their own illustrations for such articles will improve their chances of selling — and increase their income.

Modern cameras are relatively cheap and surprisingly simple to use — despite their complicated appearance and the surrounding jargon. Any reasonably intelligent person willing to read a simple instruction book can take photographs of an acceptable technical standard for reproduction. And, like literary prowess, artistic ability too is not necessary. Here too, pictures intended for publication are best if simple, uncluttered and clear. These qualities are achieved, almost automatically, by moving in close to the subject.

A further benefit from cultivating a seeing eye, to complement the writer's enquiring mind, is that article ideas can themselves be generated from pictures or sets of pictures. Rather than the usual couple of illustrations to accompany an article, it could be that the *article* is written to accompany a set of illustrations. Any such extra activities can only be to the writer's advantage. Chapter 6 looks into the whole question of illustrations for articles — how to make them and how to present them.

Getting started

There is one further aspect of freelancing — not really article-writing, but closely akin to it — that is not dealt with later in this book. And that is writing "Letters to the Editor" — intended for publication.

Many publications welcome letters from their readers and pay for all that are published: others pay only for the "star" letter. In terms of payment per thousand words — the normal freelance measure of payment — letters are often surprisingly well paid for their fifty to a hundred words.

The skills in writing such letters are: to be amusing, interesting, or provocative; and to make every word count, within a limit of about a hundred words. It is an ideal first market for the amusing personal experience or anecdote. It is an ideal training ground for the would-be article-writer. (And other people's letters are a good source of article ideas for you.)

Another advantage in trying to write "Letters to the Editor" is that they need not — indeed, should not — look professional. They need not be typed, as long as your writing is legible. And they can be on "ordinary" notepaper. The letters should look as though they were written out of altruistic interest and/or conviction, rather than with the express objective of earning a few pounds.

Some magazines will also publish — and pay for — a single photograph. Sometimes this will be on its own and sometimes illustrating a letter which is itself not paid for. These magazines are thus good markets for interesting single pictures; I have often sold photographs by writing short unpaid letters about them.

The writer's life

Finally, in this introduction, a word about the life of an article-writer. Writing is a lonely activity. No one can join you in staring at that blank sheet of paper. Few people can really help you in developing ideas — although some may unwittingly spark them off. The way you string your words together is your responsibility. You are on your own.

There are, of course, advantages to the solitary nature of the article-writer's occupation. You can write a first draft almost anywhere, ignoring those about you. You can always utilize those delays and hold-ups that are an inevitable part of modern life to think of ideas, openings, titles and anecdotes. (But make a note of your thoughts before they fade; I have forgotten innumerable marvellous ideas through omitting to write them down at the time.)

Whenever I am waiting for a train I browse through the magazines in the station bookshop. This serves as "initial sift" market research; it helps me to decide which magazines are worth buying for detailed study. And — within reasonable limits — I never mind waiting for the dentist or the doctor to catch up with my appointment time. I spend the time studying the unusual magazines in the waiting-room.

But it is all too easy for the article-writer to become lonely. You can get to feeling that no one else is suffering the same agonies of word-choice or waiting anxiously like you for the editors' decisions. To avoid such loneliness, try joining one of the many Writers' Clubs or Circles. Ask at your local library for your nearest Writers' Circle. Most circles meet regularly for helpful talks or discussions — and you meet other writers.

Another way of easing writers' loneliness is to subscribe to one of the several writers' quarterly magazines that are available. No matter how good you are at writing, or how frequently or easily you sell your work, you will always pick up useful hints from these magazines. And you will find that most of your problems are common to other writers.

From the magazines too, you will get to know of the several marvellous writers' conferences, workshops and "schools" that are held annually. There are few things so stimulating to a writer as to spend a weekend or more in the company of dozens of other writers — all bubbling with enthusiasm.

Enthused, you must then, however, return to your lonely desk. The more you write, and the more regularly you write, the better will you write. And above all, do not be discouraged by rejection slips — every writer gets them. Good, and successful, writers are the ones that keep trying.

2

What to Write About

In order to write you must have something to write about. This is obvious. Without a subject — something to say — the only recourse is to copy out the telephone directory, or whatever. And that won't sell; telephone users get their directories issued free.

What do you need for a subject? Clearly you need something that will interest the potential readers — and as many of them as possible. What, then, are people interested in? You can best answer that question by asking it of yourself. What are *you* interested in? And the answer will almost always be — in differing order perhaps — your job, your hobby, your home, your family, your health, your holiday, or just something unusual and/or interesting. Just as you find these subjects interesting, so too do most other people. The list covers a wide range of subjects, and the more interesting the subject you choose, the easier it will be to sell your article.

The golden rule

It is also obvious that, even when you have decided on a subject, you must know something about it. It would be simple for me to say that I was going to write an article about growing strawberries in a window-box. That might indeed be a good subject for an article but I couldn't write it — because I don't know how to grow strawberries. It is a subject likely to attract popular interest yet unusual enough not to have been done to death. But you must know your subject before you can write about it.

The golden rule for article-writing can therefore be stated:

ALWAYS WRITE ABOUT WHAT YOU KNOW

Ask yourself, what do you know most about? The answer will usually be your job, your hobby, your home, your family relationships, your holiday, and odd things that you find unusual and/or interesting. In other words the same list of subjects people are likely to be interested in.

Unless you are connected with the medical profession the ever-popular subject of others' health is best passed by — at least initially. (When you are a well-practised article-writer you can consider writing such personal-experience health articles as "How I cured my pneumonia by standing on my head in the snow". Before writing such articles though, think first whether you have something inherently interesting and unusual to say to others. Or are you merely indulging yourself — or even just carping? If what you have to say is not really unusual, then a doctor will say it better. There are plenty of writers in the medical profession. And the editor will buy a doctor's article about health matters in preference to yours every time.)

The same qualification about the need to say something really unusual and of general — rather than personal — interest must also apply to writing about family relationships and holidays. Few people outside of your own family circle are likely to be interested in what you said to Aunt Martha when she broke one of your best wine glasses, or how you got lost in Majorca. Make it really witty and they might — but we can't all be humorists.

Subjects of interest

We are therefore wise if we initially restrict our writing to hard, factual information about our work, our hobbies, things around the house and garden, and any subjects — including travel — that are of particular and unusual interest. In fact, to subjects about which we have some knowledge that is worth imparting.

Another factor to bear in mind when selecting individual article subjects is that most people are interested in people — that is, the human aspects of any subject. An article packed with nothing but dry factual information will be just that — dry. Add an anecdote or relate the facts to their impact on ordinary people and the article springs to life. (Bringing "life" to an article is further considered, in detail, in Chapter 4; my purpose here is merely to emphasize the interest of people in people.)

In choosing a subject to write about, think about what might interest other people in your job or hobby. An accountant could, perhaps, write a short article about how to avoid paying tax on family gifts, or how to support one's offspring through college; a housewife on preparing the garden produce for freezing, or how to cook left-overs in a microwave oven; a painter and decorator on how best to paint window frames — without painting the glass; an amateur meteorologist on the facts behind the "red sky at night" and other forecast bases.

There are many job-related possibilities — but they are not endless. The wise writer broadens his horizons.

Specialist subjects

To be successful as a writer of articles it pays to be interested in as many things as possible. A successful article-writer is a person of catholic interests. Yet, to paraphrase an old saw, *a little knowledge is an insufficient and embarrassing thing*. Make yourself knowledgeable therefore — an expert — about a limited, but ever-increasing, number of matters of interest. A catholic interest broadens the field from which you can select subjects for your articles.

But how are you to select the subjects into which to expand your interest? This must vary from person to person but perhaps I can helpfully illustrate the idea. By profession I am a civil engineer, concerned with highway planning — this has led me, deviously, to an interest in street furniture in general, and street lights in particular. My wife and I once lived in Asia, as a result of which we now collect oriental antiques — and I write about them. Our time abroad generated an interest in unusual hats — since returning to England I have extended this interest and written about curious hats. And most of all, I have developed my interest, and modest success, in writing to actually writing and lecturing on writing techniques.

In thinking about subjects in which to specialize, it is worth considering the amount of popular interest they are likely to attract. But also bear in mind that a good writer can make almost any subject interesting, by the way in which he presents his material.

One well-known British writer collected postmarks and wrote about them for many years in a wide variety of seemingly inappropriate magazines. An article illustrated with the postmarks of such quaintly-named places as Smokeless (Pennsylvania) and Coke (Virginia) sold to the specialist *Gas Times*. It all depends on how interesting you can make your subject — and how well you aim your article at the specific reader.

Article ideas

But a subject on which you are knowledgeable is not necessarily enough. You need the specific idea for the article. The idea is really just what to say about one of your subjects.

A painter and decorator could perhaps write volumes about "painting" — but magazine articles are briefer and need briefer subject ideas. He would do better with the short article suggested above — on painting window frames. This is a little snippet of a subject just right for an 800-word article. (Chapter 4 expands on the question of fitting article subjects to article lengths. There are few worse writing faults than a subject too big for the article's length.)

The problem is to generate ideas for articles. Some ideas will spring to mind as soon as you start to think about writing. Others will well up unbid at inappropriate times, sparked off by some chance remark. Ideas for new articles will be generated by reading magazines dealing with your interests. However, wherever and whenever an idea occurs, note it down: ideas are notoriously transient. Keep a notebook — an Ideas Book.

Study lots of magazines — note the ideas that other writers have developed. Try to recapture the published writer's thought process. Why did he write that article *in that way*? What made it interesting to the editor (who bought it) and to you, the reader (who also bought it)? Can you apply the same thought process to your own collection of subjects? (The consideration of sold articles — the writer's market research — is developed further in the next chapter: at this stage we are only looking at how the idea was developed.)

Old magazines too — picked up in junk shops or at jumble sales — are worthy of study. You can often safely "borrow" an idea for a new article directly from an old one that sold — and the older the better. You will only be taking the basic idea and some of the facts. The way you present your article will be fresh — and your own.

"Brainstorming" for ideas

Another way of generating article ideas is what is sometimes known as "brainstorming" — mental doodling. Take anything — an abstract thought or a trite saying; an animal, a vegetable or a mineral; or a manufactured item — and ask yourself questions about it. How was it made? Where does it come from? What does it mean? Who first said it? Who invented it? What can be made from it? How do we eat it? What does it eat? The questions keep coming; the answers generate further questions. By this process you can always produce ideas for several articles. I have never known it to fail.

Suppose you are walking along the beach; you see some seaweed — in which you have long been vaguely interested. (I haven't.) Seaweed?

- What do you know about seaweed?
- Does it only grow in the shallows? (It depends on how you define "shallows".)
- How far out to sea does it grow? (To about 200 metres depth of water.)
- Does it need air? Or light?
- How many different types of seaweed are there?

- Can you eat it?
- Isn't there something called *laver bread* that is made of seaweed? (The dictionary says *laver* is edible seaweed but it doesn't mention laver bread.)
- Where do they eat it? (Somewhere around Liverpool — I think. Can this be checked? Where?)
- Don't the Japanese eat seaweed? (I used to buy cocktail canapés from Japan, in the supermarket. They were flavoured with seaweed.)
- If it is edible, is it "farmed"? If not, why not?
- Isn't seaweed sometimes used as manure?
- Is there any connection between seaweed and ozone? (Seaside towns were wont to suggest so.)
- Is that what seaweed smells of? In any case, why does it smell?

The answers to just those questions, together with any more that arise as you discover the answers, would make an interesting factual article. I posed the questions as quickly as I could write them down and without prior thought. You could do the same.

The experienced article-writer thinks beyond the single immediate idea though. To discover the answers to the seaweed questions will involve quite a lot of research — which is discussed later in this chapter. But a lot of research for a single article can easily be uneconomic, if only in terms of your time. It is better to be able to use the one lot of research for several articles.

Let us look again at the idea. It is in fact not yet an article idea; it is just a collection of interesting snippets of information for possible future use. These need to be collected, collated and fitted together interestingly. Assuming that the answers justify the ideas, articles along the following lines could all be prepared from this one research exercise:

- "Why don't we eat more seaweed?" — a short and provocative letter for a family magazine or a daily newspaper, in summer. Also perhaps suitable for a South Coast local newspaper in summer when they are likely to be plagued with seaweed.
- "Your fertilizer grows — under the sea" — explaining how some fertilizers are derived from seaweed. For a farming magazine.
- "Eat seaweed — live longer" (or — grow slim, or ...) — a filler for a general or family magazine. If very well researched it just might work for *Reader's Digest* — but don't hold your breath.
- "England's only/first/oldest seaweed farm" — for an agricultural or "county" magazine.
- "Snorkelling through the farmyard" — a lightly factual, possibly futuristic, article about the food value of seaweed for the children's

pages of a Sunday colour supplement, or for a children's magazine with an educational bias. Also — a similar article, but re-slanted, for a women's magazine, tied to the holiday season.

- "Fat-free/Vegetarian food from the sea" — heavier, more factual article for a popular scientific magazine and/or for a vegetarian or other health food magazine.
- "Forgotten underwater shrubberies" — with underwater photographs perhaps, for a natural history magazine; possibly even for a photographic magazine.

Think how much more readily you could have generated a set of article ideas from within your own areas of interest. And remember: the more you know about your own interests, the less research you need to do for any one batch of ideas.

It will be noted that each of the articles suggested in the above list is associated with a type of magazine. Before any of the articles were written this association would be focused down to a single magazine as a "primary target". The article would be written specifically for the target magazine. The days of a general article "suitable" for a wide range of magazines, and sent on from one to the other as each rejected it, are long gone. Articles should be written for specific magazines — as is further explained in the next chapter.

It is recommended that as an article idea comes to you, you note it down at the head of a fresh sheet of paper. Turn the idea into a tentative — and for you, a helpfully reminding — title and suggest a possible market. Then, over time, while you are looking for the content material, develop the one original idea into ideas for several articles as above. Build up a file of ideas. With such an Ideas Book (or File) you will seldom if ever need to ask yourself what to write about next. (And see Fig. 2.1 for a check list of Article "No-nos".)

Check List of Article "No-Nos"
Ideas to be rejected before you start

- Don't write critical or spiteful articles — unless you can do it very cleverly or wittily.
- Don't write humorous articles — unless you really are funny.
- Don't write obvious 'reference book' articles — the editor's staff can do it better and cheaper.
- Don't write about *your* holiday — help me with mine.
- Don't write about medical matters — medical experts do it better.
- Don't write about the *obvious* anniversaries — someone else will always have got in first.

Fig. 2.1

"How to" articles

Another type of article, basic to every writer's repertoire, is the "how to" feature. If you can do something — be it making a cigar-box violin, growing strawberries in a window-box, or papering the ceiling without papering yourself — you *know*. And if you really know how to do something, and if it is something of interest to others, you can write about it and probably sell the article.

With that one qualification — that it is something of interest to others — there is a seemingly open-ended market for "how to" articles. (You may be expert at sterilizing empty jam-jars or making a cut-out doily from a £10 note, but these skills, while perhaps laudable, are hardly likely to interest a multitude of readers.) More than any other type of article though, the "how to" article needs supporting illustrations. If you have not got, and cannot get, photographs or drawings of your DIY activities at various stages, you will find it less easy to sell a "how to" article.

The "how to" article is perhaps the only type of factual article which needs virtually no research — beyond the actual activity being described. All other types of factual article depend on *research*. What does this mean to the article-writer?

Research

Research, to the article-writer, means the collection of factual material. A squirrel — could squirrels write — would be well equipped to be an article-writer. I have already mentioned — in the first chapter — that article-writing is something like 20 per cent writing, 10 per cent presentation, 20 per cent market research, 20 per cent ideas and 30 per cent research. Research is clearly of considerable importance. The article-writer does not have to advance the frontiers of all human knowledge — indeed this could often be a disadvantage. The role of the article-writer is more to bring useful information together and present it in an entertaining and interesting way to the layman.

The article-writer derives his factual information from, in random order of importance and of ease of acquiring:

— an encyclopedia
— books on the subject
— other articles on the subject
— newspaper news stories
— press releases, from large firms and government departments
— free brochures

- advertisements
- personal observations
- anecdotes recounted to you
- personal interviews
- personal notes taken from radio or TV programmes or from lectures
- museums
- reference libraries
- correspondence with people of interest
- answers to specific queries addressed to embassies, government departments, large firms, etc.

And even that seemingly never-ending list is almost certainly incomplete!

An encyclopedia is always a good place in which to start your research. As soon as I started musing to myself about seaweed, above, I reached for my two single-volume encyclopedias — the Collins Modern and the Penguin. It was in these books that I discovered that seaweed grows in the shallows and out to 200 metres depth of water.

I also possess a somewhat venerable set of Everyman's Encyclopedia which, after mention of laver bread and the use of seaweed as a fertilizer, refers the reader to the entry on the seashore — which in turn lists a section of reference books. Every would-be article-writer should have at least one encyclopedia; I recommend the Penguin one as a good starter.

Were I really interested in the flora and fauna of the seashore I would undoubtedly possess — as I do for many subjects that interest me — at least one or two introductory books about them. I would often expect to find such a book in the Hamlyn series of colour paperbacks. (I notice, from the back of another Hamlyn book, that they publish one called *Seashores* and another called *Life in the Sea* — neither of which I possess.) I would also, of course, expect there to be a fairly introductory Penguin/Pelican book on the general subject.

Remember too such inexpensive series as the Observer's Guides published by Warnes, the Shire "Discovering" books and Albums, and — although not for such things as flora and fauna — the Foyles Handbooks. And depending on the depth of my interest in the subject, I would have other general reference books.

Clearly, one is also well-advised to check what is available from second-hand book shops and from those shops specializing in reduced-price "remaindered" new books. And of course, the local library will usually have an appropriate book that can be borrowed.

Equally, over time, I would almost inevitably see one or two articles about seashore aspects — if not on seaweed exclusively — by other writers. These articles I would preferably extract from their magazines and retain. If not, photocopy them.

Similarly, in perusing my daily newspaper, there will be little snippets of information about all sorts of subjects that interest me. Not just seaweed, for that idea has only just come up, but anything of present or potential future interest. I cut them out, mark them with the source and date, and retain them. And do not neglect advertisements. On occasions, series of advertisements are featured, containing a wealth of information on subjects merely peripheral to and sometimes even remote from the advertiser's product. I collect these too.

The importance of newspaper cuttings to an article-writer is hard to over-emphasize. These little snippets of news update more learned books and articles: they also include bits of light relief ignored by the more learned, but which are *manna* to the article-writer.

Akin to press reports and advertisements are the hand-outs, press releases and free brochures often available from the most unexpected sources. London Transport has a wide variety of brochures describing things to see and do in and around London; the major banks offer tourist brochures about London — as does the London Tourist Office; wine firms issue free pamphlets about types of wine; oil companies have descriptive pamphlets for the asking. And never forget the one- or two-sheet descriptive leaflets often available for the taking in major museums: not all museum publications are high-priced. (I would certainly try the Natural History Museum in London for information about seaweed.)

Major reference libraries too (particularly the British Library at Bloomsbury in London) can be a very valuable source of information. Certainly they would have available all of the reference books listed in my encyclopedia item. Never forget the British Library's newspaper offshoot at Colindale. All British newspapers published since 1800 are available there.

Of major importance to the article-writer too — but often overlooked — is the facility whereby your local library can obtain a scarce book for you, on loan from any other library anywhere in the country. I have never yet found my library unable to locate and borrow any book that I have needed. Try them.

Personal information sources

The enthusiastic — and therefore often successful — article-writer does not limit his research to published material though. He will go out and seek personal interviews — information not yet recorded, something "quotable". Who knows, there may be a professor of oceanography living in the next street; or even just a seaweed collector or enthusiast. An enthusiast is almost certain to be willing to talk — at length — about his enthusiasm. Most people delight in talking about their favourite interest.

Personal interviews are of immense value to the article-writer. The information will be direct from the horse's mouth; it may well be as yet unpublished; it can — particularly if encouraged — be well-larded with personal anecdotes. The only hurdle to overcome is your own nervousness. Your nerves aside, your "quarry" will almost certainly be delighted to help you. A worthwhile precaution is to ensure that you have some sensible "start-up" questions. And beware of making a fool of yourself in the opening minutes — but once the conversational ice is broken this is no longer so important.

It is not advisable to make prolific notes during an interview. It can put a nervous person "off his stroke". Note down the odd key fact however — "Do you mind if I just make a note of that?" — but otherwise rely on your memory until you leave the presence. As soon as you are out, write down all that you can recall.

A portable cassette recorder, with built-in microphone, can be a helpful tool — but again, some people find them inhibiting. (A separate microphone is more "off-putting" than a built-in one). Only use a recorder if the interviewee is very willing and wholly unconcerned.

A useful tip for when you are collecting material by interviewing people is to build up "information chains". During each interview, ask your "victim" if he can put you in touch with anyone else, to take you further with the subject; obviously though, out of politeness, ask for someone on a slightly different aspect of the subject. This often pays off — or a name may be mentioned in passing, which you can pick up. Don't forget to ask for the address, or at least, the telephone number.

Of importance perhaps second only to personal interviews is information acquired by personal correspondence. If you hear of, say, an oceanographer living on the other side of the country a personal visit may not be possible. A letter can be almost as good, but it needs to be better prepared than an interview. You cannot "feed" on the answers. It is not productive to ask general rambling questions, the answers to which are in any standard reference book. Ask detailed personal and specific questions and you will almost certainly get back detailed, personal and specific answers. This is even more likely if you remember to enclose a stamped envelope clearly addressed to yourself.

Foreign embassies, government departments and large firms too will almost always answer specific — and relevant — questions most helpfully. Address the queries to the Public Relations or Press Office (PRO) at the head office of the organization. You can find most of the addresses from the London telephone directory; ask in your local library if you live away from London. When writing to PROs, a reply-paid envelope is less necessary — use your judgement on when to send one. (Never to government bodies, nor to the largest firms, but sometimes to the smaller ones who may not in fact actually employ a PRO.)

And finally, in our review of research sources, let us not forget the wealth of information provided daily by the broadcasting and television companies — including the lectures of the Open University; the proliferation of evening courses open to all; the lectures and talks given — often in the lunch break — by leading museum experts; and of course, the "one-off" lecture in the village hall. Attend, or switch on — and absorb — anything that looks even remotely interesting. And make prolific notes — no one will be put off and many speakers will be gratified by your zeal.

Notes

Notes are an important part of an article-writer's stock-in-trade. Notes should be made from borrowed books, after personal interviews, after (or, if you are very good, at) talks and lectures, and of personal observations.

Note-taking methods are a personal matter, but there are a few essential characteristics. Notes must:

- identify name — and qualification — of source and date of note-making. (For notes from borrowed books the source should include book title, author, publisher, publication date, the source from whence you borrowed it, and often the page number in the book. The ISBN (International Standard Book Number) — usually found on page iv in the preliminary pages, just before the list of contents — is also a very useful thing to record: it will enable any competent librarian to identify the book.)
- be well spaced — to enable you to annotate or amend them later.
- be set out so that their content is both clearly identifiable and easily read.

(My preference, in respect of the above two points, is to write blocks of notes on alternate half-widths down a page, and with several lines between each block.)

- as far as possible, be restricted to one subject per page — for later

ease of referencing.
● be accurate — of course.

Do not overlook — in making notes from books — the possibility of photocopying a key diagram. One such illustration can often be as good an *aide memoire* as several pages of hasty notes.

Research storage and retrieval

But what good is your widespread information gathering if it is all in a jumble? Very little. A good writer "squirrels" his collection away with care. Right from the start, file away your cuttings, your photocopies, your articles torn from old magazines, in a tidy and logical fashion.

It is a good idea to stick small newspaper cuttings on to A4 sheets of paper, several to a sheet — and preferably all on the same subject. Small cuttings get lost more readily than A4 sheets; even these have a habit of "putting themselves away" in the most inappropriate places.

I either make all of my notes on, or transpose them on to, lined A4 paper, punched for filing. Most letters from PROs, press notices, etc., are also of A4 size. So too are most photocopies and many magazines. I try to standardize all of my research material on that size — it simplifies filing.

My own practice is then to keep all papers relating to any subject in a large — A4-sized, to avoid folding — used envelope, the subject marked boldly in the top right corner. It is then quite a good idea to group together several associated subject envelopes in a card document wallet.

As a collection of material gets too much for one envelope — more than, say, twenty sheets of paper — it should be split into two or more associated envelopes, each dealing with a different aspect of the main subject. This produces a proliferation of envelopes but makes it easy to sort through the contents of any one. When I come to write an article I then extract the relevant sheets from one or more envelopes to work from. The shuffling and reshuffling of material is dealt with in Chapter 4.

Another, more sophisticated, way of storing research material for easy retrieval is to file everything in A4 lever-arch files as it comes. Each sheet is numbered consecutively, as also are the files. The files might be numbered A to Z and the pages in each file 1 to 300. The essential complement to the files is then a small card index. You would open a card for each new aspect of each subject in which you were interested; on the card, note the file and page number of each appropriate sheet of notes, cuttings, etc. This method is more efficient than mine. Were I starting today from scratch it is what I would do, but I am "too far gone" with the multi-envelope system to change now.

However you store your material, be sure that it is a logical and expandable system that you can live with. You NEED to be able to find facts quickly and easily. But your hobby is writing — make sure that it does not become "fact-filing".

Sets

Finally, your research collecting and storage will be particularly valuable if you can collect *sets* of information. Six snippets of news information about unusual hats is of more immediate value than six snippets about six unrelated subjects. The six hat items could well be enough, together with your basic general hat knowledge, to make a brief article.

The collection of sets is particularly relevant to the camera-owning writer. An illustrated article written around pictures of half a dozen unusual gates, or door knockers, or bridges, or street lights, or ... will always sell. But see Chapter 6 for what best to photograph.

You will again have noted the emphasis in the last two paragraphs on the unusual. Collect information about or pictures of the unusual: the *usual* is commonplace and won't sell; the *unusual* is uncommon and therefore interesting, and will always sell. And if the unusual is also amusing, so much the better. (I have long treasured the news item from which I learnt that the name of the Catholic Cardinal of Manila is Sin — Cardinal Sin: but so far I have not found a use for this — to me — amusing piece of information.)

3

Who to write for: Market Research

Having by now decided on a subject you feel competent to write about and duly researched it, you need to think about where to sell your article. Yes, that too comes before the writing. If you don't know for whom — for which market, or magazine — you are writing, how can you write it to meet their special needs?

As an example of the importance of deciding on your market before you write your article, think of two extremes. Visualize an article on, say, seaweed in *Weekend* or *Titbits* and a similar article in *Country Life* or *New Scientist*. It is obvious that, while the general subject matter might be common to both markets, the treatment would be very different. The article for *Weekend* might be titled — and written along the lines of — "Seaweed can affect your sex life" or "Daily seaweed ends bedroom boredom". In a more sedate magazine the same facts might be headed by "Bio-medicinal properties of English algae". The way in which the facts — and the conclusions — were written up would differ greatly.

If you were to look at any book written thirty or forty years ago about freelance article-writing it would probably suggest writing a general-interest article and then "sending it on the rounds" of a list of suitable magazines. That might have worked then; it will not work today. Articles today need to be written with a specific market in mind. There are now far fewer general magazines and many more specialist journals.

But writing with a market in mind does not necessarily mean that this is the only market for which your article is suitable. It merely means that this is the market at which you are primarily aiming. Often, if you fail to sell to the first target magazine, it is still possible to sell to a secondary market. But more of this below.

Beginners' markets

So, which magazine shall you write for? Many a tiro writer opts initially for a national daily, the *Readers' Digest*, or a Sunday colour supplement. And this is wrong.

Your object, as a beginner, is to get your work into print for pay. (Avoid working for nothing; if your work is worth publishing someone will pay you for it.) If you try to write for the big-paying prestige magazines while you are still learning the craft, you will be up against competition from the experts. There are many skilled freelance writers who make all or part of their living from writing feature articles for such magazines.

My advice is therefore, initially, to seek out the lower-paying markets: smaller magazines and local newspapers. The experts will be less interested in writing for such markets, and therefore the competition should be less. But remember that tiny fish still taste sweet to all of us; there will still be some competition. The lesser competition does not mean that the quality of your work can be anything less than your best. The lower-paying markets are an excellent training ground — their standards are as high as any.

Another approach to choosing a market is to consider the number of "sales opportunities" it offers.

A quarterly magazine made up of a dozen or more freelance contributions may be a better market than a monthly with only two or three freelance contributions per issue. Consider: $4 \times 12 = 48$ purchases per year by the editor of the quarterly; $12 \times 2 = 24$ purchases per year by the editor of the monthly. But do not be misled by this example. Not all quarterlies take more material than all monthlies. Check the opportunities for yourself; check, too, the rates of pay where you can.

Still on the broad principles of choosing a market, there are other factors to be taken into account. Although I advise against submitting your early work to the big national dailies, that advice does not apply to the regional press. Like the nationals, the regional dailies often feature freelance work in "Children's pages", "weekend leisure pages", "money pages", etc. They also take general-interest articles *with the appropriate regional flavour* for their general feature pages. And the emphasis in the previous sentence is most important. Regional dailies are as parochial about their area as are the nationals in respect of London activities and interests.

And don't forget the magazines that you yourself take regularly. If you have read *Amateur Gardening* from cover to cover each week for the last few years, you are already well ahead in market research. You KNOW what sort of article *Amateur Gardening* wants; you KNOW what the average reader wants; you ARE, in all probability, the archetypal average reader. And by now you probably know a fair bit about gardening. You will be able to

WRITE ABOUT WHAT YOU KNOW.

Choosing your market

You cannot afford to take many magazines regularly over periods of years. You must select your potential markets in other ways.

The first step is to study the current *Writers' & Artists' Yearbook*.

Look at the broad Classified Index of Journals and Magazines and work through the main alphabetical list of journals. From these two lists together you can get ideas of possible markets. These then need to be followed up.

The Yearbook entries are very helpful even though they are not enough on their own. Let us look at just one example. The 1983 entry for the leading freelance writers' magazine is:

> *Freelance Writing & Photography* (1965), Arthur Waite, 5-9 Bexley Square, Salford, Manchester M3 6DB. T. 061-832-5079. £3.50 p.a. Q. Articles and market news of interest to the freelance writer. Length: 500 to 1200 words. Payment: £8.00 per 1000 words. Illustrations: line and half-tone. Guide-lines for contributors available.

(The title of the magazine seems to have changed since the Yearbook was published — the *& Photography* is no longer on the front cover. The date is of the magazine's founding — clearly it is no fly-by-night journal. The name is that of the editor — address editors by name whenever you can. The annual subscription is then quoted, but this too has changed since the Yearbook went to press: the rates of payment had not increased the last time I sold them an article. So ... entries in the Yearbook need to be checked.)

Helpful though that entry is — as one would expect from a magazine catering specifically for freelance writers — one would be ill-advised to submit an article without further information. If nothing else, at what level of knowledge should a contribution be aimed? The offered guide-lines will help, but a detailed study of the magazine is the only sensible way of knowing for sure. (No, not "for sure" — nothing is "for sure" in the writing business.)

And, of course, *Freelance Writing* does not bear out my advice that low-paying magazines mean less competition for acceptances. Being one of the "trade journals" for freelance writers, there is inevitably much competition. But the exception proves the rule.

Lesser-known magazines

The *Writers' & Artists' Yearbook* lists several hundred British journals (and many overseas markets). The Yearbook editors acknowledge however that many magazines are not listed — usually because they are too small or too specialized to offer much opportunity to the freelance writer.

But often, as we suggest above, these small and/or specialized magazines are just the ones the tiro writer should aim at. Within your specialism or occupation you will know, or can get to know, of the small specialist journals. (And don't ignore the many free magazines — most pay their writers, and often quite well.) The prudent freelance writer also spends time looking at the magazines on display in book shops. He looks out particularly for new publications, of which more below.

The other ways of learning of little-known magazines are by keeping your eyes (and ears) open — particularly in waiting-rooms — and by reading "market reports" in freelance writing magazines. (A comprehensive writers' market information service is provided by the *Contributors' Bulletin*, the sister publication of *Freelance Writing*.)

Samples

Having identified a number of magazines — and perhaps newspapers — as potential markets for your work, you need to get sample copies of them. Yes, copies — not just one.

Before you go out to buy all these samples though, pause a while. How many are you going to get? I could go through all the steps I have outlined above and sort out several dozen potential markets for myself. But could I *cope* with that number of markets? Certainly not, at least initially.

Suppose I were able to write one acceptable article for each of the thirty or forty markets I have selected. When could I write the next one for the same market? It is far better to build up a steady relationship with a few editors than to provide a lot of editors with "once-only" sales.

The advantages of building a relationship with any magazine are:

- Knowing your work has been good in the past, the editor will tend to look favourably on each new submission from you. (But only while you keep up the same acceptable standard of reader-interest and writing-quality.)
- When the editor needs to commission a special article, your name may come to the editorial mind. (Having had one two-part article accepted plus a couple more submitted on spec and still being considered, the editor of a magazine otherwise new to me telephoned to commission an article. (See "Hallowe'en", Chapter 5.) The subject was totally new to me, which meant some frantic research. But it was a sure sale from out of the blue and it had the bonus of opening up a new subject for me.)
- Your overall work is reduced by the need only to update your market research. (Remember the breakdown of freelance article-

writing into: idea — 20 per cent; subject research — 30 per cent; market research — 20 per cent; writing — 20 per cent; presentation — 10 per cent. Selling repeatedly to the same magazine changes these figures to something like: 20, 30, 5, 20, 10 — a saving of fifteen per cent of your effort. And a commissioned article obviates the need for thinking of an idea — a saving of a further twenty per cent.)

For your first efforts therefore, narrow your choice of "target magazines" down to just two or three. If possible, let these be totally different types of magazine. Ideally, choose one or two magazines that accept general-interest articles and one or two dealing with your special interests. (More than one specialist magazine only if you have more than one specialism — not two on the same subject.)

These two or three targets permit you to think of two or three different articles; which can, of course, be different treatments of the same subject. Restricting yourself to two or three magazines keeps down the cost and the effort of market study.

(When you have produced an article of saleable standard for each of your three initial targets you can research alternative markets. Search then for magazines with requirements as similar as possible to each of your initial targets. You will not always find such markets. When you do though, they can be offered articles that you are quite sure are saleable, but which have been rejected by your initial target magazine. This can easily happen if an editor has recently dealt with your subject in his magazine; however good your article, it would not then be accepted. Editors will sometimes — very occasionally — tell you the reason for their rejection.)

Buy two or three sequential copies, or every other issue, of your finally narrowed-down choice of two or three magazines. Some magazines of your choice may not be on sale at book stalls. In such cases, write to the editor — a typed, businesslike letter — explaining that you hope to write for him and asking for two or three recent sample copies. Ensure that you enclose sufficient payment to cover cost and postage.

It is often worth taking this opportunity to ask if the magazine has a "contributors' guide" that you can be given. (Only a few British magazines offer such guides; many American magazines offer very comprehensive guidance brochures.)

What to look at

You now have to *get into* the magazine of your choice. Not "be published by", although that is your final objective, but get into the

32

mind of the editor. For what sort of reader does he produce the magazine? Your object will be to write just what that reader wants, and expects to read, in that magazine. That is what the editor will buy.

You also need to ascertain how much of the magazine's contents are the work of freelance writers, and how much is staff-written.

The first things to look at when studying a magazine as a market for your work are not the articles themselves, but rather:

- the advertisements,
- the contents page, and
- the illustrations.

Studying advertisements

Advertising is a highly sophisticated profession. The advertising agencies know just who are the readers of each magazine in which they display their clients' wares. They will, if necessary, vary their product presentation — their advertisement — to suit the readers of a particular magazine. By studying the advertisements you can work backwards to an appreciation of the reader at whom they and the magazine are directed.

There are few advertisements in the *Amateur Photographer* for home film-processing kits. There are many advertisements however offering commercial film processing. This seems a good indication to me that most *AP* readers are not much interested in developing or enlarging their own film and pictures. I question whether an article on film processing would sell as readily to the *AP* as one on, say, picture composition. (Certainly I would not try one, although they do appear in print in the *AP* from time to time.)

Do not look merely at the whole-page advertisements. Look carefully too at the small "two-column-inch" boxes, usually grouped together under a "Market place" or similar title. Some magazines even have a "Job Market" section which is particularly useful to you. The sort of person they are advertising for is the typical reader.

Advertisements for personal stair lifts clearly indicate an older reader. Similarly, advertisements for "Stop your child's bed-wetting" suggest a family readership in the twenties to thirties age-range. Building Society advertisements too can be helpful — they can be directed either at old income-seekers or at young mortgage-deposit-savers. Either way, they tell you a lot about the readership.

Note particularly — but do not automatically shy away from — magazines that contain either no advertisements at all or only single-product advertisements. These are usually house magazines, sometimes produced just for the prestige, less frequently now as tax-losses, but sometimes just to keep staff informed of "company policy". The "company policy" mouthpieces seldom take outside contributions, and you will be wasting your time studying them. The prestige magazines, however — of which the Halifax Building Society's *The Home Owner* is a fine example — welcome freelance contributions and sometimes pay quite well for them.

Apart from the contents of the advertisements, it is worth looking at the quantity of advertising. Free magazines, which have proliferated recently, rely wholly on their advertisers for their livelihood; the editorial matter may be little more than a "come on" for the advertisements. Minimal and/or poor editorial matter will, however, eventually be self-defeating; readers will not bother to read it or the adjacent advertisements. The better free magazines pay well for editorial material, to ensure a welcome for the magazine and a noticing of the paying advertisements.

But no editor with a lot of advertising, whether his magazine be free or expensive, will be prepared to upset his advertisers. An article "knocking" a product or type of product represented in the advertising pages will seldom be accepted — no matter how good the article may be. Save such thoughts for consumer-research publications.

Studying editorial pages

Consider now the Contents page of a magazine. Frequently this will separate out for you the regular columns from the special features. Regular columns — either staff-written or a long-standing series written by a regular freelance expert — come under a variety of headings. They can be called, simply, "Regular Features", "Departments", "Regulars", or even "Also". They may sometimes be identifiable as the only items without a writer's name or an explanatory sentence.

It is important to take note of the regular features because these deal with areas of interest where you stand little or no chance of selling your work. If an editor is committed to buying an article every month from an expert on, say, money matters, he is unlikely to buy one from you on family budgeting. (I fell into that trap just recently myself. I had failed to recognize a column as a regular feature.)

The Contents page will also identify the amount of fiction the magazine carries. In the context of selling articles, the pages devoted to stories are lost to you. The titles of the stories may, however, give yet another indication of the readership.

The titles of articles too, and the accompanying "blurb" tell you something about the readership. Are the titles flamboyant, brash and "pushy"; or are they fairly staid? Are they up- or down-market?

Even the space and importance devoted to the Contents page is of interest. Some magazines omit or restrict the contents listing — their readers will not bother to read advance listings. The readers are probably regular buyers of the magazine, and like to dive straight in. They know what to expect. These magazines — *Weekend* and *Titbits* spring immediately to mind — sell by action-packed internal pages and a startling cover. Other magazines, designed perhaps for the slightly more serious readers, attract purchasers through their Contents pages. *Amateur Photographer*, for example, always strikes me as that sort of magazine.

Leave now the Contents pages and flip through the rest of the magazine — looking at the pictures. Photographs of beautifully-prepared food dishes on elegantly laid tables might suggest an up-market middle-aged female readership. Pictures of scantily-clad girls suggest a readership of around-twenty-year-old girls — or men of any age. Pictures of vintage cars, exotic far-away places and a mix of older people and younger children, all in the same magazine, suggest a readership of fairly affluent grandparents. (*Choice* is a prime example of such a magazine.)

Thus, you can quickly get a "feel" for a magazine's readership — from the advertisements, the Contents page, and a quick flip through the illustrations. Now turn to the articles themselves.

Studying the articles

By sorting out the staff and regulars' features from those supplied by freelances, you have considerably reduced the work of studying the articles themselves. At this next stage in the market-study process you want to look into:

- article subject — not specific, more generic. (Thus, not "Interview of Billy Bloggs, megastar of stage, TV and radio", but just "personality interview". Billy Bloggs himself is now unimportant; the editor will not take another article about him for some years.)
- article length. Count the words in ten lines and divide the result by ten to give words per line. Count the number of lines in a full page free from illustrations, or make allowances for the "lost" lines. Multiply words per line by lines per full page to give total words per page. Use this as a first, rough, basis for estimating overall article lengths — by assessing areas of print as half a page or whatever. Get a feel, too, for the lengths and numbers of paragraphs in some of the articles. (We shall come back to word counting in more detail in Chapters 4 and 5.)

- illustrations. Check the number of pictures accompanying an article. Were they essential to the sale — as in a photo-feature — or merely to liven up the page? (The latter were probably put in by the editor.) How much colour is used? Notice how many pictures are upright and how many are horizontal — and how many are of people. (And again, we shall return to the subject of illustrations in Chapter 6.)

You will note that even now we are not really studying any one article in great detail. We come to this in the next chapter, where we pull to pieces an article chosen as a model.

A market-study example

To exemplify the approach recommended above for studying a magazine, let us look at a single specific issue of *SHE*. (Not a market that I would recommend for initial attempts at selling, but a good one to study for later "attack".)

The issue of *SHE* that I am studying has 132 pages including the cover — the bright, eye-catching front cover being page 1. Of those 132 pages, 62 pages consist of advertisements, a surprising third of which are double-page spreads. Nearly a half of all the advertisements are whole pages. It is clearly a market favoured by "big" advertisers. The advertisements themselves can be categorized, by pages:

shoes (including children's shoes)	6
other clothes (women's only)	3
cigarettes	7
alcohol	3½
foodstuffs	10½
perfume and other beauty preparations	9
personal hygiene products	7
miscellaneous	16
	62 pages

From that review — and from the content of individual advertisements — we can tell that, unsurprisingly, the magazine is directed at women. But the children's shoes advertisements bring out the fact that some of these readers are parents. The alcohol advertisements and the clothes displayed in all of the advertisements suggest that the readers are better paid than shop assistants or pool typists. This socio-economic judgement is borne out by the perfume ads, which are all for good quality "middle-price-range" products.

And generally, the advertisements suggest an air of independence and "moderate liberation".

Turn now to the Contents pages — yes, two pages. The first is a tempting photo-preview which undoubtedly attracts readers, but is of little help in market study. The second Contents page is a detailed listing in sequential order. It too is not ideally designed to meet the special needs of freelance article-writers. The most striking feature of the contents listing is the repeated use of the magazine name in the titles: "Tell *SHE*"; "*SHE* puts her feet up"; "*SHE* Beauty"; "Miss *SHE*"; etc.

Setting aside for the moment the identifying of staff and freelance contributions, I flip through the pages, looking at the illustrations. Most are spectacular in one way or another — many by being of startlingly unusual subjects. One that caught my attention was the back view of a young woman wearing jeans with an almost completely cutaway seat: the picture was made even more spectacular by including a bearded Jewish man walking past, wide-eyed.

There are many pictures of girls, usually girls doing things. One girl is just sitting on the floor, but there are others putting on a sari, inspecting a car engine, and back-packing in America. There is a girl driving a train and another helping to police Los Angeles. Almost every photograph in the magazine is of people — and at least half of the pictures are upright. Other than in the fashion pages, almost every picture is in black-and-white. And there are a lot of line drawings scattered about the pages — all very slightly jokey.

Once again, the image of the reader is of a youngish, but definitely not teenage, woman with an independent attitude to life. A sort of "I can do anything I want to if I try" person. The sort of person who would not take kindly to being patronized, but could laugh at herself when appropriate.

I turn now to the literary contents of the magazine. There are 70 pages of features: 40 pages that I think have been produced by staff or by regular contributors and 30 pages by freelances. Of the twenty freelance articles, most (14) take up one page or less, four spread across two pages and two are even longer. (There are also some whole pages of photographs, a short story and even one poem.)

The article subjects are particularly interesting. Virtually all are of equal interest to male readers as to the obvious female readers.

The articles cover a variety of subjects — several being personal experiences treated with a trace of humour. Another type of article appearing more than once is the interview — not necessarily of a celebrity. One fascinating report is of interviews with several "ordinary" people, recording their housework likes and dislikes.

Another article type which appears twice is the "How to" article:

there is a very detailed article on how to make your own wine; another on how to tend miniature *bonsai* trees. I noted also that no subject seems to be barred — there are features on politics, spouse-swapping and religion, all cheek by jowl with each other.

The three-quarter- and one-page articles are all about a thousand words in length. The balance of the page, as much as thirty per cent, is filled by pictures, associated comments or advertisements. The thousand-word articles are usually divided into around twenty paragraphs; the average length of paragraph is therefore about fifty or sixty words. (The longest paragraph I noticed was ninety words long and the shortest, twenty.)

The above market-study exercise has given me a very good idea of the sort of article that can be sold to *SHE*. And I think that I know the reader quite well. But, I repeat, *SHE* is not the best magazine for a beginner to try writing for. A smaller, less competitive, market would be better initially. (I deliberately chose to dissect an initially unsuitable magazine — you must do your own market study, not take my word for it. And I have only touched the high spots of what you learn by detailed market study.)

I have only pulled one issue of *SHE* to pieces. That is not sufficient. When doing it "for real" I would repeat exactly the same process but with two or three recent copies. That was why my advice above was that you should buy two or three sample copies. The content of one issue may be unusual: three issues will sort out the "funnies".

Sell to the editor

And now, before leaving the marketing side of freelancing, let us look at the buyer. (Never forget, you are selling — and it's a hard, buyers' market.) The buyer is not, as far as you are concerned, the reader; your buyer is the editor. He buys what he thinks his readers want. If the editor changes, so too will the buyer's policy.

Picture then the editor, who has to produce a newspaper or magazine every publication day; he has many blank pages to fill. He probably couldn't, and certainly doesn't want or intend, to write all the material himself. Nor can he usually afford full-time staff to write it all. So he buys work from freelance writers.

Once it is known that an editor is in the market to buy articles, he will be inundated with material. Much of it will be totally unsuitable. (Too many unsuccessful freelance writers do far too little market research.) Therefore, when he does find fresh, interesting material, geared specifically to his needs, he seizes on it. He builds up a stockpile of suitable material.

When the editor starts to plan the next issue of a magazine, he starts with his regular features; then he perhaps has one or two essential pieces to put in, features tied to the publication date or to recent news. After that he looks to his stockpile. What will fit in? "That one, that one and that. Fine — a nice mix." He is content.

Now suppose that he has no stock of suitable material. He may then have to accept the best of the material that just happens to be submitted at that time. The alternative is to write something himself. Whatever he does, somehow he has to fill the pages. If his store is well-stocked he can be "choosey"; if the cupboard is bare he will want to fill up as soon as he can.

The purpose of the above description is not to attract expressions of sympathy for the poor editor. It is to demonstrate your opportunities for salesmanship.

As soon as you have sold your first article to an editor, send him another one. Make sure that your second offer is every bit as good as that just accepted. If that one too is accepted, the editor will begin to recognize your name. Your work will be looked at favourably; the editor will hope that you are again offering him something he can use.

And one day, you may get a phone call from the editor to ask you to write an article on a subject of his choice. An editorial commission!

One other hint follows from our description of the hard life of an editor. Keep your eyes open, and watch the market reports such as the *Contributors' Bulletin*, for news of new magazines. The editor of a new magazine will have no stockpile; he will be interested in developing new ideas; he will welcome writers with something new to offer.

But, a warning, new magazines are sometimes short-lived. You may not get paid for published work if a magazine closes down. Your accepted but unused work in the stockpile will, if you are lucky, be returned.

And finally, remember always the importance of market study. If your work is what an editor wants, he will buy it. This suggests a second golden rule of article-writing:

KNOW YOUR MARKET

And know it well.

4

The Article Content

You have your idea, you have done the research, and you have studied the market. Now you can start to think about the writing side of the business.

You are going to write an article: "A short piece of non-fiction writing intended for sale." (*The Concise Oxford Dictionary* defines an article as a "literary composition (other than fiction) forming part of a magazine etc. but independent of others".) My definition is much the same, but shorter — and more realistic.) Consider that definition: an article is NOT the same as a school essay; it is NOT the same as an academic thesis; it is NOT the same as a technical report. The essential difference is that an article has to attract a purchaser. Put another way, an article has to *persuade* the reader to read it. If it is unlikely to interest — and therefore attract — the reader, no editor will buy it. And if it does not get bought, it does not get read.

The way to persuade a reader to get into your article is to grab him straight away. Then, once he is hooked, don't let him go until you finally round off your article at its end. We come on to those essential parts of an article — the start, the middle, and the end — later in this chapter. For now, consider how you are to handle the subject in the given space.

Your market study will have told you that the editor of your initial target magazine prefers "your sort of article" to be perhaps eight hundred words long. Have you got an 800-word subject? In detail, this is something you can only learn from experience, but in general, the fitting of subject to length is not too difficult. You would not, I am sure, try to summarize the history of China in 800 words; that needs at least a book, and probably many books. But I have successfully related — in 550 words — how one early Chinese emperor ordered a particular jade artefact made to aid him in his worship.

Clarify therefore, before starting to write, just what your article is to be about. Then confirm to yourself that you can do justice to that subject within the space available. It is no use offering even the most marvellous 2500-word article to an editor who never takes anything longer than 800 words.

A discipline often adopted by lecturers and other speakers is to define their objective before they start. This might well be in such terms as: "Having heard this lecture/talk, the listener should be able to print his own forged banknotes"; or "... brew a cup of tea"; or "... understand how to prune his roses". It is often worth applying a similar self-discipline to article-writing. It may help to ensure a consistency of approach throughout the article.

Planning the article

Having mentally clarified the purpose and the subject of your article, it is now possible to plan it in some detail. Start with a blank sheet of paper. At the top, write the subject. This is not yet the title, merely a working guide.

Next, working from the notes and papers that are the product of your research, list the facts and fancies that are to make up your article. The list, at this stage, will be in no particular order: it is just a list. Review the facts, etc. Have you enough to really fill an article of the length you plan? If not, can you get more?

Remember, though, that an article cannot be merely an assembly of unsweetened facts. The facts must be made palatable. The reader must be interested. So perhaps you do have enough factual material after all. Perhaps what you lack is the jam filling that makes the doughnut? Can you find some unusual, and therefore interesting, snippet of information, or an amusing story, to leaven the factual lump?

Once you are content that you have enough material — or better, a little too much, so that you can be choosey — you are ready to shape your material to a plan. Here I cannot help you much. Only you can decide on the format or structure that you should adopt; the order in which you present the facts and fancies on offer.

You can plan your article so that the facts follow each other in historical order. Or you can arrange them as a story, with historical flashbacks. "How-to-do-it" articles are of course best structured in a sequential form. But other practical advice articles are sometimes best structured with the most important advice first — or last. (In a recent article on how to take saleable photographs, I listed the basic rules of good photography in what I considered to be their order of importance.)

The most important thing about an article structure is that it be logical; that the facts fit together sensibly. And, of course, that they retain the reader's interest.

Using a model

Just as budding artists learn their craft by copying the works of the great masters, so too can writers. In essence, for the tiro writer it means — at least initially — modelling your work closely on similar published work. It does not mean copying a published article. Apart from the ethics, the subject will not sell twice in the same place. But working to a model will help you to offer work of a style acceptable to the editor.

Find an article in a recent issue of your target magazine, of the length you propose to write and on a similar subject. Pull that article to pieces. This is the same process as the general market study, but in more detail.

Read your model article very carefully. Note the lightness, or otherwise, of the writer's tone. Note particularly the first paragraph; this is all that many people will read. Note the number of separate "stories" that are included in the whole. Count the total number of paragraphs, and the number per "story". Count the number of words in each sentence and in each paragraph: and this time, literally count every word. Look carefully too at the words themselves — how long, or "difficult" are they?

You may think I am obsessed with counting numbers of words. I have been accused of this before. Every successful writer counts words though — I am perhaps more thorough than others. Initially at least, I commend my approach to you. Unless you note every word, it is easy to miss the important differences between styles.

In front of me I have an article published in the general-interest magazine *Titbits*. The title is typically provocative: "Get 'em off — and get results" — but the article is really about successful ways of making a protest. The article is 580 words long in 22 paragraphs. The longest paragraph is 48 words long, the shortest is a 10-word single sentence. The average paragraph length is only 26 words. No paragraph contains more than four sentences — and many paragraphs are only one or two sentences long. Some sentences are quite long — one is 34 words in length; but many are very short. One sentence is only 6 words long, and the average overall is only 15 words per sentence.

There are eight "stories" in the article, each told in two or three short paragraphs. The stories are:

- thirty mothers breast-feeding their children in a crowded High Street shop, to demonstrate the lack of alternative facilities for this;
- a nude Italian girl asks for a bath at the mayor's house — the only house in the village still supplied with water;
- a man strips off his clothes in the social security office — to draw attention to his need for a clothes grant;
- the owner of a faulty chair sits on it, on top of his car, outside the defaulting shop;

- a farmer returns rubbish dumped in his field to the garden of the "dumper";
- an artist dumps manure outside a newspaper office — for the use of their art critic;
- a housewife goes on strike and pickets her own house until the family agree to help with the housework;
- a man complains to the council about the distractingly "sexy noises" coming from the next-door bathroom.

It would be pointless to offer the editor of *Titbits* another article about unusual methods of protesting for the next few years. But if you have an idea — and the knowledge — for a 500-600 word article on another suitable subject, your article can be modelled on the protest one.

You will need to write in sentences averaging about 15 words in length. These sentences should build up into paragraphs no longer than 50 words, averaging about half that length. (There is more about sentence and paragraph lengths in the next chapter.) You need about eight "stories" to fill out your article. The "stories" need not be as titillating as those in the protest piece — but in a magazine like *Titbits* this would always be a welcome bonus.

Constituents of an article

Think now of what constitutes a magazine article. We have already defined it as — even more briefly than before — "short saleable non-fiction". Its constituent parts contribute to its saleability. They are:

- the title,
- the opening paragraph,
- the middle,
- the closing paragraph,

and perhaps

- the illustrations (see Chapter 6).

Each of these constituents has a role to play. They all work together, in an integrated whole. Each part is worthy of examination in detail.

Titles

The title of an article is the first thing anyone notices. Sometimes, if you are lucky, it is featured on the front cover of the magazine; usually it is mentioned on the Contents page; invariably it heads the article itself, in bold print. The title catches the roving eye of the "flip-through" bookshop browser. And a particularly good title may sometimes influence an editor's decision on whether or not to accept your article.

A title therefore needs to have impact.

A long title can often have all the dynamism of a large bowl of semolina pudding. The browser will give up half-way through. Ideally, try for a short, snappy title; one that will immediately capture the casual interest. But ... sometimes a long title will be gripping. There are no firm rules. As a general guide though, most people agree that short titles are preferable to long ones.

Ideas for titles are all around you: listen out for catchy, snappy, "phrases-of-the-day". (I gave one of my articles the title "Write On" — but it did not sell.) Study the titles of other published articles — a slight twist, together with a changed subject, might fit them admirably for yours. Consider too, the use of alliterative phrases — phrases made up of words with a common beginning.

Think about titles whenever you have a spare moment — while waiting for the train, or for the five-o'clock whistle. Titles themselves often lead to article ideas: you will sometimes think of a marvellous title, and then write an article to go with it.

Most titles fit into five broad categories. Consideration of the categories can itself often help you to come up with a good title: (Not all of these examples are of my own titles — yet; but listing them has already given me an idea for another article.)

- the label — the simplest title of all, and often the most effective; ("Jade — China's most precious stone"; "How to survive at meetings"; "Make your own ...".)
- the question — with which can be linked the provocative statement;
  ("You think you are a good ..."; "English men make better ...".)
- the quotation — or better, the twisted quotation;
  ("Evil is at the root of much money"; "More than one wolf at the door".)
- the exclamatory statement, or "screamer";
  ("Here be dragons!"; "How it feels to almost die".)
- the pun — and it need only be a weak one at that.
  ("Cashing in on history" — about old coins; "Pants for every body".)

The editor will not always agree with your idea of a good title. As long as he buys your article, this is his prerogative. He may replace your weakly punning title with a simple label. Or he may think up a more provocative title. It is always interesting — and often instructive — to observe such editorial changes.

Opening paragraphs

While the title may be the lure, the bait, that attracts the flip-through browser, the opening paragraph of an article is the hook that draws him in. The first paragraph is all that the casual reader will read — unless it grips him, and his interest, very firmly. The first paragraph must be punchy; it is the "taster"; it must go with a bang.

Like the titles, opening paragraphs can be of five basic types, somewhat similar to the title categories:

- the simple statement — the opening equivalent of the label title;
  ("What gold is to the European, jade has always been to the Chinese. They value jade not only for its beauty, but also for its hardness and its seemingly endless life.")
- the question — usually provocative;
  ("Are your pockets bulging, your handbags unclosable, and your drawers overbrimming — with certificates, statements and sales slips? Do you really need to keep all this paper? Or are you hoarding it unnecessarily?")
- the quotation — usually "straight", rather than as in the "twisted" title;
  ("'Ming umbrella-stand sells for £250,000.' We have all seen such newspaper reports and looked wistfully at the favourite — but cracked — willow-pattern plate hanging on the kitchen wall.")
- the "shocker" — the equivalent of the exclamatory or "screamer" title;
  ("Ten children will die on the roads of Britain in the time that it takes you to …")
- the anecdote — the story approach.
  ("The editorial specification said 750 words plus illustrations. 'Fine,' said I. 'That'll be easy.' Although I knew the subject well, I still scribbled out the points I wanted to make …")

It is not necessary to use an opening paragraph of the same basic type as the title. Sometimes it works, sometimes it does not. And the market for which you are writing will influence your choice of opening. The more flamboyant the magazine, the more they will welcome flamboyant openings.

Remembering that the opening paragraph has to hook the uninterested reader, there are two qualities to aim at in writing it. The opening should seek to involve — to draw in — the reader: use the word "you" whenever possible. And the opening should ideally tell the reader something new and interesting — or make it obvious that what follows will be of interest.

The opening paragraph should be short. Short paragraphs are more punchy than long ones; they get to the point quicker; they are easier to read. The flip-through browser will seldom bother to "taste" a long opening paragraph at all. As a rule of thumb, try making the first paragraph half the length of the average. (If your model has an average paragraph length of fifty words, write your opening about twenty-five to thirty words long.)

Middle paragraphs

The reader's attention firmly seized by the opening paragraph, it is now up to you to hold that interest throughout the article. You must "play the reader along" until he gets to the end.

The body of your article should be full of interesting information — but it must not read like a catalogue of facts, or an extract from an encyclopedia. The interesting information can be provided in the form of facts, statistics, anecdotes and quotes.

We have already discussed, in Chapter 2, the sources of the material that will go into the body of the article. And we have noticed how, in our sample article, the facts are assembled in a number of "stories". It is part of the craft of the writer to present the facts and statistics in an interesting manner.

Statistics and numerical facts are important — but dull. The writer can add a little sparkle, a little interest, to them by comparisons. Don't just say that, for example, the Malaysian State of Sabah is 29,000 square miles in size. Illustrate that by telling the reader that this is little more than one-tenth the size of Texas, or three-and-a-half times the size of Wales. (The choice of comparison will depend on the market at which you are aiming.) In illustrating the numerical facts, however, do not neglect to quote the facts themselves. Include the actual size as well as the comparison. And avoid describing something merely as "very" — very big, very small, etc. Always quantify — say how big or how small.

Anecdotes too are important: and good anecdotes are never dull. But you may not have been able to collect enough anecdotal material — as recommended in Chapter 2. In such a situation there is nothing wrong in producing your own anecdote. An anecdote is no more than a fact or an experience expressed in story form. So long as your facts or experiences are accurate, they can often be embroidered into a more useful format. Try not to do it too often though — made-up anecdotes can lack the freshness of reality.

I knew that small pieces of jade were being sold very cheaply in a nearby town. I had bought some; that was a fact. I needed a female-oriented anecdote. I invented a fictional housewife who went gift shopping, reporting her conversation with the dealer from whom she bought some cheap jade pieces. Here was no invention of facts, merely a "fictionalization" of them. Within the limits of probability, this is perfectly acceptable.

And don't forget that the ideal anecdotes are those relating your own mishaps. You are the ideal person to appear in your articles as "the stooge", the "fall-guy". You, best of all, can show how to avoid the same mishap recurring; the reader will identify with you. (Notice how I have used my own experiences in this book to demonstrate possible slips.)

Quotations, like anecdotes, help to make an article come alive. By their nature they represent the views of other people — people perhaps with whom the reader can identify. They add the weight of someone else's views — someone perhaps well-known — to the comments of the writer.

Do not imagine that all views and opinions quoted in an article were collected at first hand by the writer. Quotations used in articles can indeed come from personal interviews, but some come from other sources. You can re-quote from interviews published elsewhere; you can quote from a source's published articles and books (but keep such quotations short — say fifty words at most); or, very usefully, from published books of quotations. In books of quotations the hard work has been done for you; the nuggets of wit and wisdom have been sorted out by subject.

Looking in one of my own books of quotations, I find, for instance, that George Bernard Shaw — of course — made a typically witty and relevant comment. He said, "I often quote myself. It adds spice to my conversation." When you are as well known, you can try this — until then, quote others. All quotations add spice.

Closing paragraphs

When you come to the end of your article, you need to round it off conclusively. There is nothing worse, in an article, than just stopping. That just looks as though you are exhausted — devoid of further facts or sufficient ability: that must never be so. Ideally, you need another startling fact, another "bang", on a par with the opening paragraph. If you have used the best of your available material in the opening paragraph, try to save the next-best item for the end.

If you haven't got anything spectacular with which to end, then try for some other way of rounding off the package. Bring the reader back to the purpose of the article; remind him how, having read the article, he can now better cope with something. On try for a mildly witty conclusion. (I ended up a solid factual article about the need to keep paper — bills, statements, etc. — by disclaiming any ability to advise on how to keep paper money. That, I left to the reader.)

And because, in its own way, the closing paragraph is as important as the opening, strive as before for impact. Keep the length of the final paragraph as short as the opener. This will help.

Writing methods

And finally, because everyone is always interested in the unimportant personal details, how — physically — should you write? This must be a very personal choice; I can only tell you what I do. I write all of my articles in longhand on alternate lines of narrow-lined A4 hole-punched paper. I get the big "Jumbo" pads that the multiple stationers sell for student use. (And I buy up stocks whenever I see them on "Special Offer" — usually at the beginning of term.)

Writing on alternate lines provides just about enough space for the many changes that I make to the first draft. My writing is very small. It also allows me to partly polish my work (see Chapter 5) without rewriting whole pages. I then do my own typing — no one else could interpret the mess that my revising often causes — completing the polishing process as I type the final version. Figure 4.1 shows a typical page of my manuscript drafting. It will give you an idea of how I polish as I go along. And Figure 7.1 (see p.76) is the final typescript.

Some writers work directly on to the typewriter, then revise and polish the typed draft before retyping. I find it easier to work with a pen because I often change the words as soon as I have written them down. (I mouth the words too, as I write; this helps me to "write as I talk" — for which, again, see Chapter 5.) Beginners may need to rewrite their first draft completely, but that apart, I recommend my approach. At least try it: I know it works, for me.

As to *when* to write, I don't think this matters; the important thing is to write often and regularly. I write — or work at the associated tasks — for about an hour each evening. And I spend several hours at my desk on Saturdays and Sundays.

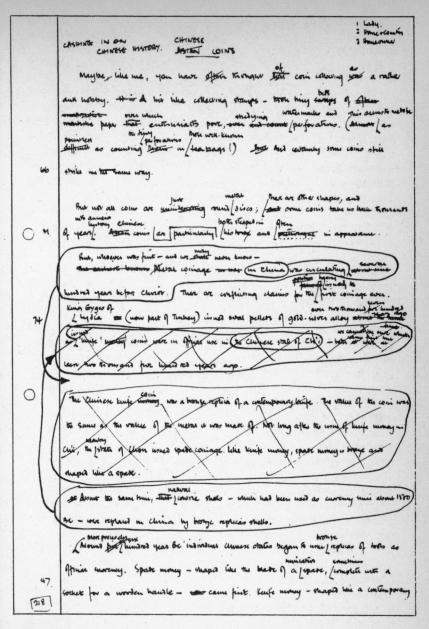

Fig. 4.1
A typical page of my own drafting — the start of the article which is shown as typescript in Figure 7.2.

49

5

Stringing the Words Together

The task of the writer is to communicate. Unless he conveys his message to the reader, his writing is all a waste of time. The writer communicates with words: words strung together in sentences, building into paragraphs and linking together to form the whole. Words make sentences make paragraphs make articles.

Each and every word must be chosen with care. Each word must be a "communicating" word — not one written to impress the reader. Unless you communicate, you will not sell. Editors buy "interest" — not "cleverness".

Writing — the sort that will sell — is hard work. If anyone tells you that he just sits down and the words flow easily, he is either an unpublished writer or a born genius. When you are writing for sale you must at all times ponder on whether the typical reader will understand. And not just understand, but be really interested by and enjoy your writing. Even if the reader understands, but is not gripped, he will often not bother to read. That means that you must take care with every word that you use.

Style

There are few, if any, fixed rules about writing. And if I were to be so rash as to propound one, someone is certain to break it — successfully. Even much of the grammar that was taught at school is no longer so important as it once was. Note for instance how frequently writers — not just me — start sentences with "And" or "But". And how often do you see an infinitive beautifully split? (Editors sometimes correct my split infinitives — most no longer bother.)

The nearest thing to rules on how to write, that I can offer, is the writer's ABC. Let your writing be:

A — accurate — which is a matter of careful research. If you make a mistake, someone is sure to notice it, and write to the editor. If that happens often (at all?) your credibility will wane, and with it, your sales.

B — brief — concise might be a better word, or "don't waste words".

C — clear — and simple. Use "easy" words in easily-read sentences.

Leaving aside the question of accuracy, the research base for which was investigated in Chapter 2, the two remaining qualities are brevity and clarity. And these two qualities go very neatly together. Good concise writing is usually clear.

This chapter opened with the concept that words make sentences make paragraphs make articles. Everything starts with the words — so shall we. It is obvious, if you stop to think about it, that your reader will find it difficult to understand any word that you yourself had to look up in the dictionary or Thesaurus. The average reader will not enjoy struggling over difficult words. And he will automatically classify any long unusual words as "difficult".

Try not to use words in your article-writing that you would not use in your day-to-day speech; and if you must use the dictionary or Thesaurus, seek out the best-known, the short and easy alternative. It comes back to communicating rather than seeking to impress the reader with your literary skill. A useful rule of thumb is to stop and think hard before using any word that is more than three syllables long. (In this test, ignore those relatively simple words made long by the use of endings such as -ed, -ment, or -ly; and those words which are the result of joining two simple words together.)

Mark Twain expressed his preference for short words in a delightfully business-like way: "I never write 'metropolis' for seven cents, when I can get the same price for 'city'."

But don't carry too far the search for short simple words. If the RIGHT word is a long one, use it.

As the words build up into sentences, keep these short too. There is nothing wrong with a long sentence, except that it is hard to write well. It is all too easy to get carried away with balancing clause and counter-clause; and the "beauty of the well-turned phrase". It is also easy to omit the verb — or put in one too many. A short sentence is easier to write. All you need is a subject, an object and a verb. If a short sentence is easier to write, why struggle to write a long one?

Short sentences are also easier to understand. An American study showed that when sentence lengths reach more than about twenty-five words, only ten per cent of readers can understand them. (I only just got that thought into a maximum length sentence.) Unless I am working to a model with shorter lengths, I write to an average sentence-length of sixteen words — and a maximum of twenty-five. But occasionally I go over that top limit. And note that I suggest working to a much shorter average. With a maximum of twenty-five and an average of sixteen, there have to be some very short sentences too.

(The average sentence-length in the previous paragraph is fifteen words — with two sentences knocking on the maximum length.)

A useful discipline is to think out the whole of each sentence before you write it down. Of itself, this approach will usually lead to shorter, simpler sentences. Who — other than perhaps a Jane Austen — could hold a complex sixty-word sentence in their mind without putting pen to paper? Another useful idea is, once written down, to read each sentence aloud — or half-aloud, under your breath. Reading your work back to yourself in this way ensures that you don't write anything you would have difficulty in saying aloud.

An American management writing *guru*, Robert Gunning, expresses this readability concept as the advice, "Write as you talk." This is ungrammatical but helpfully explicit. And it fits in well with the ethic of Don Marquis, who said: "If you want to get rich from writing, write the sort of thing that's read by persons who move their lips when they're reading to themselves."

Paragraphs too should be concise. Not necessarily short, but as short as they can sensibly be constructed.

Ideally, a paragraph contains a single aspect of a subject; a single thought plus any associated explanation. Sir Ernest Gower puts this well when he says that "every paragraph must be homogeneous in subject matter". He further explains that while an over-long homogeneous paragraph may be sub-divided, it is wrong to combine several short paragraphs into a longer paragraph of several thoughts.

The reason for advocating shorter words and sentences is to improve the clarity and to make the reading easier. The basic logic of shorter paragraphs contributes less to the cause of easy reading. Rather, short paragraphs are a presentational matter. Look at any old book on your shelves, or visualize an ancient newspaper. With long paragraphs the printed page was one solid block of grey. Breaks between paragraphs relieve the greyness. Shorter paragraphs increase the number of gaps in between; they increase the white space; they make the pages LOOK more attractive — and easier.

As a further rule of thumb, when writing articles, I generally aim at an average paragraph length of about fifty or sixty words. And I work to a top limit of about eighty words. (Books are different: paragraphs can be a little longer. The column width is greater in a book than in a magazine; this means less depth of type for the same length of paragraph. In books I aim at an eighty-word average and sometimes stretch well over a hundred for the maximum.)

Do not, though, write all of your paragraphs the same length. That would be boring. Vary the length of your paragraphs; in this way you impart an extra interest, a varying rhythm, to your writing. It looks better and it reads more easily.

The first sentence should state the main thought contained in a paragraph. Subsequent sentences should then develop, and expand on, that initial theme. Ideally, the last sentence then rounds off that paragraph's thought. And because short sentences have greater impact than do longer ones, there is much to be said for making first — and last — sentences short. But of course, to adjust sentence lengths slavishly and deliberately can easily spoil the natural flow of your writing. All I suggest is that you bear these thoughts in mind.

The flow of your writing will be improved if you endeavour to link consecutive paragraphs together — not physically, but in thought. These links can be achieved by starting a new paragraph with a passing reference to its predecessor. This may not always be possible, but where it is, paragraph linking makes the reading more easy.

Examples of linking phrases with which paragraphs can begin are:

- "But these are not isolated cases..."
- "Yet if you look around..."
- "Not only does..."
- "But that may never happen."
- "And..."

So far, we have ignored the matter of punctuation. But this is no longer the difficult matter that it once was. Short sentences need nothing more than a full stop. No problem there. Nor is there any great problem in adding the occasional comma to a longer sentence: so long as it is only occasional. It is only in the longer sentences — which I recommend you eschew — that other punctuation marks are needed.

Avoid the exclamation mark. Other than very rare use of it is the mark of an amateur. Your words should serve the same purpose. The question mark is easy to use. It is the mark of a question. The only difficult punctuation marks are the colon and the semi-colon.

The colon is almost a full stop: it is a means of linking two short, separate, but associated thoughts. It is also the introduction — without a dash — to a list. Other than in listing, it is best avoided.

The semi-colon is half-way between a comma and a colon; each phrase separated by a semi-colon should be as complete as a sentence; a semi-colon should always be capable of being replaced by a full stop. Use the semi-colon with great care — or not at all.

Checking up

In the previous section I have stressed the importance of short sentences and paragraphs. To keep a check on the lengths and on the balance of one sentence or paragraph with another, it is necessary to count words.

For the beginner, until you acquire a "feel" for sentence and paragraph lengths, I recommend actually counting every word. After writing lots of articles and more than a dozen books I still count every word that I write — one by one. Each time I reach the foot of a page of manuscript — about 250 to 300 words usually — I count the words I have written.

I count by paragraph, marking the total for each in the margin. As I count, I take mental note of sentence lengths; I hold the count at the end of one sentence in my memory until I reach the end of the next; if the "second-sentence-extra" is more than twenty, I stop and reconsider; if the sentence seems to go on for ever, I stop and rewrite. (But — as then — I would count a semi-colon as the end of a "sentence".)

While I am counting, I think about comparative length, and rhythm. Does that paragraph consist only of several long sentences? Can I fit in one short one, to leaven the pill? Even though no sentence is "too long", how is the average? Have I made the most important point in the first sentence, or have I buried it? Are the paragraph lengths too similar? Are they all too short, or — more often — too long? How is the overall length going — compared with the "model" and the material I have yet to use?

At the end of each page I also check quickly back on the actual words I have used. Are there many long words — or any "over-long" ones? Have I slipped into the use of jargon that my reader will not understand? Any such faults, I correct before I move on to the next page. I have begun to round off the rough edges of my writing. But I haven't yet started polishing — that comes later.

So... by dint of much effort, we finally make it to the end of the article. Check first on the overall length. It will almost certainly be too long: longer than your model; longer than the subject deserves. This is no bad thing. It allows you room to polish your writing.

Polishing

Everybody's work needs polishing. There is very little writing that cannot be "tightened up"; there are very few writers whose work is not occasionally unclear; there is always a possibility that an imprecise word has slipped in. To weed out all the "less-than-good" writing, you must review your work. (Refer back to Figure 4.1 for an example of how I polish, and then look forward to Figure 7.1 for an idea of how some of it turned out.)

Read the whole article through to yourself again, aloud, but in a hushed whisper. This process will identify the phrases that you thought looked good on paper but which cannot easily be spoken aloud. It should also identify the long words and the jargon which you may use without thinking, but that others may find unusual.

Whilst reading the article half-aloud to yourself, watch out for sudden warm flushes of literary pride. If you feel particularly pleased with the way you have worded a section of the article, of its sheer literary merit (and your skill)...cross it all out and rewrite it. If you have such feelings of pride it is almost certainly not simple enough — and that must always be your aim. (If you yearn to display literary skill, try writing long philosophical essays: but don't waste anyone's time trying to sell them.)

Having read your article through half-aloud, and made your written work more akin to everyday spoken English, look again. This time re-read silently.

Reconsider every word. Is it necessary, or is it "padding"? Cut out all padding. Is there an "interesting" word that you found in the Thesaurus or the dictionary? If so, try to find a more everyday word: if you had to look it up to make sure of the meaning, your reader may well not understand it. And he won't bother to look it up. Consider too whether you have qualified the unqualifiable. Examples such as *very* unique, *slightly* pregnant and *absolutely* dead demonstrate this often overlooked fault.

Another common form of padding is the unnecessary sentence lead-in: "I think that..."; "In order to..."; "And, of course,...". Such phrases are little more than a written "er — um — er" pause. They don't carry the reader forward at all, they are redundant, and they should be struck out.

Check your words to make sure that you have the meaning — and the spelling — correct. Time and again, when writing, I find that a word I propose to use does not mean exactly what I thought it did. This is usually when I am going for a longer word that I would use in speech — in other words, when I am breaking my own "rules". Time and again too I find that my spelling needs to be checked. Yours will too — no matter how competent you are sure you are. Use your dictionary often.

Should you need to emphasize points in your writing, do this by your choice of words and the structure of your sentences. Under-lining is usually the hallmark of an amateur writer. And a technical point: underlined typescript — if left thus by the editor — will appear in print in *italics*. These are not particularly emphatic in appearance and should be reserved for foreign or unusual words, and for book and magazine titles.

Working through your manuscript, "polishing out" the difficult phrases and the unnecessary words, you may decide that you must rewrite the whole article.

Do not despair. For a beginner this is no bad thing. The rewrite will be much improved, much "tighter". For a more practised writer it is still not unusual — certainly I rewrite many individual paragraphs. And my finished drafts are a maze of alterations.

When you have revised, rewritten and polished your work until you are satisfied with it, read it through aloud once again. Does it still sound natural, or have you polished away all the liveliness — all of your style? If so — rewrite it. And finally, count the words yet again. Is the overall length now about right? (It needs to be within say fifty words of your model for any article of a thousand words or less.)

A worked example

Let us look now at how I went about writing the article on Hallowe'en that appears as Figure 5.1.

I had approached the editor of *Townswoman* for samples of the magazine — for which I paid — and had mentioned that I was thinking of offering her several articles. One suggestion, of a commemorative feature on the socialist suffragette Sylvia Pankhurst, took her eye and she asked for it urgently. I provided just what she wanted, quickly and in time. My professionalism paid off: a few weeks later the editor telephoned me, out of the blue.

"I want six hundred words about Hallowe'en," she said. "Tell the readers what it is, how it came into being — all that sort of thing." "But I don't know anything about Hallowe'en," I said. "Then you'll enjoy doing the research, won't you?" was the cheerful response. "I want the copy by..." Clearly I couldn't escape — not that I wanted to — so I had me a commission. I have had a few other wholly unprompted commissions in my time, but they don't come so frequently that they can be passed up. And the editor was right; I did enjoy finding out. I really did not know anything about the subject — everything in the article was new to me.

I collected the material from various books on my own shelves, from a couple of books found for me by my friendly local librarian — and from asking everyone within earshot what they could tell me. I had none of my preferred batches of newspaper cuttings to fall back on. But research techniques are not what we are looking at in this chapter. We are considering how to write.

My submitted article was entitled "Hallowe'en — the night when time stands still". But the editor changed that, as you can see. (I thought my title was quite good but the payment cheque amply compensated me for its disappearance.)

The opening paragraph of my submission was:

For all its present emphasis on demanding a hand-out with "Trick-or-Treat" threats of mischief, Hallowe'en is not an

₂₄ original American custom. Even the pumpkin lantern-faces are
₁₅ of Irish origin — a development of their 'Jack-o'-lanterns'.

(The numbers to the left are the number of words in each sentence.)

I had wondered how to start the article off and decided to take a well-known feature of Hallowe'en — a possibly unpopular one with *Townswoman* readers too — and debunk it. It is partly a "simple statement" opener and partly a "shocker" — to use the categories listed in the previous chapter. In any case it was effective: the only editorial changes were to substitute "Despite" for "For all", and to take out the capitals I had used in "Trick-or-Treat" (I had been inconsistent.)

My second paragraph — short and, I thought, perhaps mildly provocative to a possibly conservative readership — was run into the first when it got into print. (To my mind, running the two paragraphs together reduced the "separated" emphasis that I was seeking with the second paragraph.)

> Like many other Christian festivals, Hallowe'en — All Hallows Eve, the eve of All Saints' Day — has its origins in Celtic ₂₁ paganism.

Being part of the refutation of the American origins, this amalgamation was perfectly sensible editing. Both of my paragraphs were part of "the same thought". And the editor explained to me later that she couldn't really spare *the space* for short paragraphs. (Remember the reason why I advocated them?)

Note that in my first two paragraphs I used a total of 60 words in three sentences: an average of 20 words per sentence. I brought my average down in the next few paragraphs.

The next three paragraphs in my submission were all about the Celtic festivals and the Celtic calendar. Again, more or less the same "story" or thought, so it was not unreasonable that the editor ran the three together. (In my original, handwritten draft, I had myself written the first two as one, decided it was too long, and split it into two.)

> ₉ The Celtic year was based on the farming calendar. The year
> _{5.4} began on November 1: the start of winter; the end of the growing
> ₈ and harvesting time; the time for mating the sheep, and
> ₁₃ slaughtering livestock surpluses for winter food. The turn of the
> year was celebrated in the great festival of Samain (or Samhain),
> ₂₀ the Lord of the Dead.

Notice here how the first brief sentence makes the main point,

The witching time

It's Hallowe'en time again and Gordon Wells tells us about its pagan origins

DESPITE ITS present emphasis on children demanding a hand-out with 'trick-or-treat' threats of mischief, Hallowe'en is not an original Amercian custom. Even the pumpkin lantern-faces are of Irish origin — a development of their 'jack-o'-lanterns'. Like many other Christian festivals, Hallowe'en — All Hallows Eve, the eve of All Saints' Day — has its origins in Celtic paganism.

The Celtic year was based on the farming calendar. The year began on November 1: the start of winter; the end of the growing and harvesting time; the time for mating the sheep and slaughtering livestock surpluses for winter food. The turn of the year was celebrated in the great festival of Samain (or Samhain), the Lord of the Dead. The other great Celtic festival was that of Beltine (or Beltane), held on May 1 to celebrate the end of winter. The festival of Samain was a solemn, often frightening, occasion; that of Beltine was a time of rejoicing. The eve of Samain, the end of the old year, was thought to be a 'between' time — belonging neither to the old year nor to the new. It was the night when time stood still. Then, neither time nor the boundary of the nether world was well defined. The 'natural' laws were in suspension and demons, ghosts and witches wandered at will. It was a night when wise men stayed home and locked their doors.

One feature of the festival of Samain was the lighting of bonfires. These were intended to help the sun survive through the long winter. Meanwhile, they also served to protect the people from the denizens of the nether world. The bonfires of course survived, not just at Hallowe'en but now, more commonly, a few days later in commemoration of the infamous activist Guy Fawkes. But Hallowe'en fires themselves continued to burn, on burial mounds and hill-tops, right through until the latter part of the last century. At Fortingall in Scotland, an annual bonfire was lit on an ancient burial mound until 1924 — when the custom was finally stopped because it interfered with the grouse.

All Saints' Day — to honour those saints without their own special day — was originally established in the seventh century as a May festival. But the awesome festival of Samain was still celebrated with too much pagan enthusiasm to be long ignored by the Christian church. In the eighth century All Saints' Day was transferred from May to November. Samain became Hallowe'en.

Hallowe'en remained a night of mystic fear throughout the Middle Ages.

Grotesque changes

Around the end of the 17th century, the festival of Hallowe'en began to change. Villagers now donned grotesque masks and represented themselves as ghosts and demons. They went from house to house, singing, dancing, and collecting offerings of appeasement originally left for the real ghosts. These masked 'guisers', as they were called, then led the unseen evil spirits off to the outskirts of town and away. It was then only a short step — of a century or so — to involve the children, with costumes and door-to-door collections. By the beginning of the present century, Hallowe'en was largely dying out in England. (The Irish and the Scots continued to celebrate it.) The English Hallowe'en was largely absorbed into the Bonfire Night celebrations.

Hallowe'en flourished in America after it was taken there in the 1840s and their 'trick-or-treat' customs were developed. Brought back by US servicemen in the 1939-45 war, the American way of Hallowe'en has since then been regaining popularity in England. Few houses today are safe from occasional 'trick-or-treat' visitations.

The Lord Samain would no doubt turn in his grave. If only time would once again stand still, for just one night — or perhaps it does?

Fig. 5.1
A worked example. A published article of mine, about Hallowe'en. (Reproduced from The Townswoman October 1982 by kind permission of the Editor.)

elaborated in subsequent sentences. Note too the use of punctuation in the second sentence. "The year began on November 1:" introduces several elaborations explaining that statement. Each explanatory phrase ends with a semi-colon, the list having been "introduced" by a colon. And the whole construction effectively produces a lot of short "sentence-equivalents", thereby reducing my average sentence length (to under 14 words) and making the paragraph easier to understand.

The next two of "my" paragraphs are part of the same general thought. They again express the main thought in each first sentence and help to keep the average sentence-length down.

The other great Celtic festival was that of Beltine (or Beltane),
22 held on May 1 to celebrate the end of winter. The festival of
10 Samain was a solemn, often frightening, occasion; that of
8 Beltine was a time of rejoicing.

The eve of Samain, the end of the old year, was thought to be a
"between" time — belonging neither to the old year nor to the
27.8 new. It was the night when time stood still. Then, neither time
13 nor the boundary of the nether world was well defined. The
"natural" laws were in suspension and demons, ghosts and
14 witches wandered at will. It was a night when wise men stayed
13 home and locked their doors.

In the second of the above paragraphs, notice how, while the main
point is made in the first sentence, the second sentence carries
emphasis — largely by its short sharp message "It was the night when
time stood still". Within these two paragraphs the average sentence
length is only fourteen words — and not one word is a long one.
My next two paragraphs dealt with Hallowe'en bonfires: I had
separated them because of the time difference; the editor once again
ran them together because of their content.

12 One feature of the festival of Samain was the lighting of bonfires.
These were intended to help the sun to survive through the long
13 winter. Meanwhile, they also served to protect the people from
15 the denizens of the nether world. The bonfires of course
survived, not just at Hallowe'en but now more commonly, a few
days later, in commemoration of the infamous activist Guy
25 Fawkes.

But Hallowe'en fires themselves continued to burn, on burial
mounds and hill-tops, right through until the latter part of the
22 last century. At Fortingall in Scotland, an annual bonfire was lit
16 on an ancient burial mound until 1924 — when the custom was
12 finally stopped because it interfered with the grouse.

Notice how I linked the two original paragraphs by the "But
Hallowe'en fires themselves continued to burn…" I then followed
that up with the nearest thing to an anecdote that I could manage. (It
was also a veiled social comment: the old customs had to give way to
the sport of the gentry.)
I was a little worried about using the word "denizens" in the first of
these two paragraphs. It is not a word in day-to-day use — but I

decided that the readers of *Townswoman* would be unlikely to find it difficult or distracting. I would not have used it in an article for *Weekend* or *Titbits*.

My next paragraph dealt with the religious takeover of the Celtic festival. Although relatively short, it stood alone. And the next paragraph too, even though very short, needed to stand alone to give the impact that I sought. The editor agreed with my judgement.

All Saints' Day — to honour those saints without their own special day — was originally established in the seventh century
23 as a May festival. But the awesome festival of Samain was still celebrated with too much pagan enthusiasm to be long ignored
22 by the Christian church. In the eighth century All Saints' Day
13 was transferred from May to October. Samain became
3 Hallowe'en.

Hallowe'en remained a night of mystic fear throughout the
11 Middle Ages.

Notice particularly that final sentence in the first of the above paragraphs. Its very shortness gives it urgency and impact: *Samain became Hallowe'en*. No ifs, no buts: just a bald statement of fact. And the three-word sentence balances the three longer sentences that preceded it. The average sentence length in that paragraph is only 15 despite two sentences each containing twenty-plus words.

We now come more up to date — which is acknowledged by the editor in her sub-heading. Again, she ran my next two paragraphs together. Both deal with the changes in European customs, so the running together was not unreasonable.

Around the end of the seventeenth century, the festival of
14 Hallowe'en began to change. Villagers now donned grotesque
12 masks and represented themselves as ghosts and demons. They went from house to house, singing, dancing, and collecting
19 offerings of appeasement originally left for the real ghosts. These masked "guisers", as they were called, then led the unseen evil
21 spirits off to the outskirts of town and away.

It was then only a short step — of a century or so — to involve
23 the children, with costumes and door-to-door collections. By the beginning of the present century though, Hallowe'en was largely
15 dying out in England. (The Irish and the Scots continued to
10 celebrate it though.) The English Hallowe'en was largely
11 absorbed into the Bonfire Night celebrations.

In those two paragraphs I used a most effective link, "It was then only a short step..." (It was so effective that the editor joined the paragraphs together.) In the first paragraph I toyed with the need to put quotation marks around "real ghosts", for how does one differentiate? But I decided that this was unnecessary — which is another useful rule of thumb for applying to punctuation: only punctuate where it helps the reader's understanding.

Note the sub-editing in the second paragraph. The word "though" has been deleted twice. On reflection I think the first should have been left in, but the deletion of the second is an improvement — I had used it unnecessarily.

Having started the article with the American involvement in Hallowe'en celebrations I came back to it in the penultimate paragraph.

20 Hallowe'en flourished in America after it was taken there in the 1840s and their "trick-or-treat" customs were developed.
23 Brought back by US service men in the 1939-45 war, the American way of Hallowe'en has since then been regaining popularity in England. Few houses today are safe from
11 occasional "trick-or-treat" visitations.

The Lord Samain would no doubt turn in his grave — if only
23 time would once again stand still, for just the one night. Or
5 perhaps it still does?

Notice the short punchy final paragraph — and observe how the editor has varied my punctuation. The exchange of the dash after "grave" for a full stop is a definite improvement but I still prefer my full stop after "night", to the editor's dash. The phrase ends the article with just a hint of Hallowe'en fear.

The editorial changes that were made were all relatively minor; clearly the editor didn't think there was a lot wrong with my writing style. And such changes are the editor's absolute prerogative. Banish any ideas that your choice of words and style is in any way sacrosanct. The paymaster has the last word.

And finally, in this example, see how it meets my own standards of easy readability. The article is 617 words long, very close to my 600-word target. The average sentence length is under sixteen words: if I count phrases bounded by semi-colons the "sentence length" comes down to just over fourteen. The longest sentence unbroken by a colon or semi-colon is 27 words long; most of the longer sentences are only 22 or 23 words long.

Even in the printed version, despite paragraph-linking, the average paragraph length is only 77 words; as submitted, it was 47 words. There are only a handful of words more than three syllables long; to the best of my belief there are no "difficult" words at all. (As already mentioned, "denizen" is one that I would hesitate to use in everyday speech, but it was right in this context.)

Throughout, I wrote simply and concisely — as though I were talking to a friend over the garden fence. I avoided any literary pretensions and just told what I knew. Given the material and the ideas, anyone can write like this — and sell the result.

6

Illustrating your Articles

Look at any magazine or newspaper, and think back to the market research chapter: many articles are illustrated. If you can offer an editor a selection of relevant illustrations together with your article, the editor's job is made easier. You may thereby sell more articles.

Pictures will help your articles to sell; conversely, if you are already selling photographs, articles will help to sell your photographs. Do not be worried about illustrating though — many articles are sold without illustrations. Illustrations are merely a bonus to article-writers. There are, in any case, many organizations which will provide a writer with useful photographs — often free of charge.

If you are interested in illustrating your articles, but have no photographic expertise, this chapter will set you on the right lines. Photography today is easier than it ever was. As we shall see, you need do little more than compose the picture and release the shutter. (Competent photographers may also find much that is new in this chapter.)

Types of picture

What sort of picture is bought by magazines? The way to find the answer to that question is to look again at various magazines.

It is immediately obvious that most published photographs are black and white pictures. Of course there are colour pictures in many magazines; but these are often on the "staff-written" pages such as the fashion and cookery features. Almost all "general interest" articles in almost all magazines are illustrated in black and white. So...you must learn to take black and white photographs.

Overwhelmingly too, most pictures published in magazines and papers are of people or things relevant to the article they illustrate. Outside of the news pages of the daily papers, there are few "news" pictures. Outside of the editorial page — and even there only very occasionally — there are almost no "artistic" pictures.

If a leading politician has a spectacular accident right in front of your camera, by all means take a photograph or twenty — and rush to a newspaper office with the film unprocessed. Do not, however, try to compete with staff photographers at, for instance, a sporting event. They get the vantage points to photograph from, they have the equipment and the processing facilities to meet the editor's deadlines. You cannot compete.

Similarly, do not strive to take the sort of photographs that win camera club competitions. Put aside ideas of picturing back-lit drops of rain on a cobweb-draped twig. Don't try too hard to be artistic. Even if your photography does eventually extend into taking pictures to sell for their attractiveness, you will probably be most successful taking naturally attractive landscapes.

And, last of the "do nots", do not bother to seek out spectacularly attractive girls to adorn your photographs. Although the daily papers are often full of such pictures they are usually commissioned — or really advertisements. "Girlie" pictures are not needed as illustrations to general interest articles.

So...forget news pictures, club-competition-winning pictures and pictures of scantily-clad girls. Your article illustrations will often be still-life pictures: pictures of gates, bells, antiques, etc. You will mostly be concerned with the interest of the subject. A picture of an amusingly misshapen carrot will always sell. So too will a picture of road signs or advertisements that become amusing by virtue of their setting. (A signpost to "World's End" alongside a "No Through Road" sign is the sort of juxtaposition that will almost always sell.)

A good market for the single picture of the curious carrot or of the silly sign is the "Odd Snap" spot found in many magazines. Watch out for such opportunities, they often pay quite well.

Another large proportion of your general interest article illustrations will be pictures of buildings, trees, castles or street-scenes. There is no overwhelming need for your picture of such scenes to be "different". An editor will usually prefer a conventional picture of Blanktown Castle to, for instance, a close-up of a broken battlement against a stormy black sky. (But you might sell the two pictures together — so don't pass up any different or unusually attractive shot you "see".)

The balance of the photographs suitable for illustrating articles will be those of people or animals. Readers like pictures of people: people *doing something* — even just dozing in a deckchair. And pictures of animals will often outsell "people pictures" — particularly if they are a wee bit unusual.

In a nutshell then, the photographs that you take to illustrate your articles must be of interesting subjects. The subject of the photograph is of far more importance than the artistry. And whenever possible and appropriate, some human interest should be included.

Equipment

Before we go on to discuss how to take a saleable picture, let us consider the equipment needed. You need not bankrupt yourself. The basic equipment is just a camera and a length of film. It is seldom worth processing your own films or enlarging your own pictures — certainly it is not essential.

First then, the camera. There are many cameras that use film smaller than 35 mm wide; there are still some that use the large roll films. The smaller the film, the more it has to be enlarged for reproduction in a magazine or paper — and the greater the enlargement, the more the defects in your photographs will show up. Yet there is merit in small size — portability if nothing else. A 35 mm camera is the best compromise for the article-writer.

You can buy a good-quality, new, 35mm single-lens reflex camera from the proceeds of only three or four article sales. What sort of camera would that be?

A single lens reflex (often referred to as SLR) camera has a viewing system which, by a series of reflecting surfaces, enables you to look through the lens itself. You compose and focus the picture on an internal screen which shows, more-or-less exactly, what will appear on the film. The focusing will usually be aided by a magnified and/or split-image central spot. (The latter merely requires you to align the two halves of the picture.) Most SLR cameras today offer automatic exposure setting. Once the camera controls are set for the film in use, just press the shutter release and the film will be correctly exposed. As I have already said, it is difficult to go far wrong in photography today.

The SLR camera will use 35 mm film which is sold in cassettes of 20 or 36 exposure lengths. Care is needed in loading the film into the camera and when all the pictures have been taken the film has to be wound back into the camera. But these are simple processes. The camera will record images on to the film, to become negatives or slides 24 mm × 36 mm in size.

It is possible to change the lens on a 35 mm SLR camera. Supplied with the camera will be a 50 mm (or thereabouts) standard or "normal" lens. The size of the lens — the 50 mm quoted for the standard lens — is a measure of its focal length. The greater the focal length, the more the image is magnified and the smaller the angle of view encompassed. Thus, the 50 mm standard lens purports to capture an image equivalent in angle of view to that of the human eye. A 35 mm or smaller lens is known as a wide-angle lens — because it covers a wider angle of view. Lenses of 85 mm or longer focal length are classed as long-focus or telephoto lenses; they magnify the captured image in proportion to their length. (For example, a 100 mm telephoto is sometimes called a 2X telephoto — the image is double the size of that obtained from the standard lens.) Initially though, stick to the standard lens alone. I managed for years with no other lenses.

The best reading matter on how to use your new SLR camera is the instruction book supplied free with the camera. It will tell you all you need to know — and you need to know all it tells you. The more familiar you are with the operation of your camera, the less you have to think about when using it. You must be able to concentrate on the picture — not on the machinery.

Gadgetitis is endemic among photographers but should be resisted — as far as possible. Apart from your basic camera, the only extra that you really need is a UV (ultra-violet) filter — to protect the lens. The UV filter has a marginally beneficial effect on the pictures you take, but more importantly it protects the lens itself from finger-prints, or worse. Depending on the lens on your camera, you may also want to buy a "+1 dioptre" close-up lens — but only if you need to take a lot of close-up photographs.

If you do not feel capable of coping with a quality SLR camera, you can get an even simpler one. Some simple "compact" 35 mm cameras avoid even the need for focusing. They offer click-stop zone focusing and fully automatic exposure. The fixed lens in a compact camera is usually a wide-angle; this reduces the need for critical focusing. Compact cameras are marginally cheaper than the average quality SLR camera — you pay for their simplicity. They are only recommended for those who don't want to know at all about photography, for whom they are ideal. (They are also a useful second camera for the enthusiast; their compactness means they can be taken anywhere.)

Should you, in time, expand your photographic interests and hope to take many colour pictures for sale, then you might consider a second, larger, camera. Colour transparencies (slides) on 120-size roll film are more saleable in some markets than are 35 mm colour slides. The most suitable, "value-for-money", camera for 120 colour is a twin lens reflex 12-on-120 camera; there are several still on the market. Another alternative is to track down an old 120-size folding camera, such as a Zeiss Super Ikonta. Renovated, such a camera will produce ideal 8-on-120 colour transparencies.

Film and processing

As already explained, virtually all of your photography — other than your "holiday happy snaps" — should, at least initially, be in black and white. (You will have to look carefully at the racks of film on sale to find this "old-fashioned" medium. The popular photographic market is geared to selling and processing colour negative film, film that produces colour prints.)

Most of your pictures will be taken without rush or panic, in good light, often out of doors. You can therefore standardize on a moderate speed film that will produce pictures of relatively fine grain. I recommend that you use film of around 100 to 160 ASA speed. Most film manufacturers offer a film in this range: the best known are Kodak Plus-X and Ilford FP4.

If you do decide to take 35 mm colour photographs to accompany your articles — perhaps a travel or nature article — you must take slides. It is still almost impossible to sell negative colour photographs (the amateur's standard film); editors demand transparencies. Not only do they demand transparencies, they virtually insist on one type of 35 mm film — Kodachrome. You may like other brands of film but the editor is used to Kodachrome and may reject any other film merely because it looks different.

The processing of Kodachrome is done by Kodak — who better? — and is allowed for in the purchase price. This is not the case with black and white film. Most mail order film processors — the firms that slip mailing envelopes through every door in the summer — do not handle black and white processing. The multiple chemists' shops will accept black and white film for processing, but they are not wildly enthusiastic about it. But look at the small advertisements in the photographic press. There are plenty of small firms who offer specialist black and white mail order processing. Experiment to find a processor who suits you and stick with him.

Taking photographs

You have your camera, it is loaded with film as instructed in the book, and now you want to take pictures. But you have never used a "real" camera before. Your past experience is limited to taking "happy snaps" with an Instamatic.

Before you dash out to take your first set of pictures it may be useful to look at your old "happy snaps". Or if you haven't any, think of those that you have been shown by your friends. And this time look, or think back, hyper-critically. What are the faults of most "happy snaps" — apart from the sheer quantity? In random order — for it is difficult to decide which is the least important — most beginners' faults are:

- a 'messy' picture, the subject of which is not obvious;
- the subject too small in the picture ("That's Aunt Dollie there at the back by that bush.");

- "heads and tails" cut off;
- a "fuzzy", unsharp picture — due to subject movement, camera movement, or improper focus;
- always horizontal ("landscape") pictures, even for vertical ("portrait") subjects.

Now consider the picture needs of editors. We have already remarked that editors are not particularly concerned with artistry. What then do they want? They simply want the illustrations they use — and buy — to be:

- big,
- clear,
- sharp,

and if possible,

- lively.

A comparison of those two lists demonstrates the problem. Now let us consider the solution.

The first rule for taking acceptable, saleable, photographs is simple. It is far too often forgotten, yet it is the most important rule of all. It is:

DECIDE ON THE SUBJECT

If you are taking a picture of a church weathervane, you must concentrate the camera's attention on the weathervane. You should not — for this purpose — photograph the weathervane complete with steeple, church, graveyard and lych-gate — however attractive the resultant picture may be. (Photograph the "church complete" by all means — it sounds attractive — but then store it away until you want one of the church, not the weathervane.)

"Concentrate... on the weathervane." Do this by filling the picture with weathervane. Filling the picture with a subject perhaps thirty metres above the ground is of course easier said than done. It could entail the use of a telephoto lens, which you should not (yet) invest in. So, when you get your negative back from processing, order an enlargement of the weathervane alone. With the 100-160 ASA film recommended, such part-enlargements are quite possible.

Had you been photographing a small antique, a dog with a bone, or the "church complete", it would have been easier to fill the picture with the subject. The second rule of saleable photography is now obvious:

MOVE IN CLOSE

Don't worry overmuch about placing the subject artistically within the bounds of the picture. The editor is quite likely to trim off "all that waste space". Just move in close and make sure that the subject fills the picture.

Getting close to a subject is of considerable assistance in ensuring that the picture is clear. There can be no doubt what the subject is. But not every subject is suitable for ultra-close portrayal. You may have defined the subject as "a person looking at the landscape". (And to include a person in a landscape adds valuable human interest to a subject often difficult to photograph well.)

In taking pictures such as the person admiring the landscape or a fisherman mending his nets, it is essential to watch the background. Nothing makes a picture less *clear* than a confusing background. In the heat of picture-taking however such details are often overlooked. Who, in their right mind, would ever photograph the classic picture of the tree growing from the top of a subject's head? Yet such pictures abound — because the photographer forgot at just the wrong moment.

If you seek to take photographs that will sell, you must never forget the background. The third of our rules can therefore be:

WATCH THE BACKGROUND

The person-plus-tree is an extreme example of a poor background. The best and simplest backgrounds contrast, rather than merge, with the subject. That way the subject automatically stands out, clearly. Simple ways of achieving this include:

- squat down so that you are looking up at the subject — this will usually provide more sky in the background. (It doesn't work so well in built-up areas though; the buildings themselves may be "fussy" at all angles, and a tilted camera makes buildings appear to lean over.)
- stand on something so you look slightly down at the subject — making a grassy field or the shimmering sea your background. (The high viewpoint is also suitable in towns: cobbles particularly make a fine pictorial background — and foreground.)
- a bit more technical — adjust the camera exposure settings to open up the aperture (by increasing the shutter speed): this will mean that the camera can be focused more selectively on the subject, throwing the background out of focus. (Notice how often the television cameramen use this technique of selective focus.)
- by contrasting lighting. Picture, for example, a musician on stage, under spotlights, against a black wall of faces. Or, if a subject is such that a silhouette is acceptable — such as a picture of a statue

perhaps — photograph it against an attractive but paler sky.

The fourth rule of saleable photography is:

GET IT SHARP

Few things detract more from a picture than the fuzziness of camera or subject movement, or of incorrect focusing. And it can sometimes be difficult to tell which of these three is the cause of a fault. Yet all can be avoided very simply.

Both camera and subject movement can be cured by a faster shutter speed. (This can also, as we have seen, help by throwing the backgrounds out of focus.) Use a shutter speed of at least 1/100 sec. whenever possible — and hold the camera as steadily as you can. Brace the camera against the neck-strap or hold it against a wall or shelf whenever possible. If you still suffer from camera or subject movement, go for an even faster shutter speed.

If a subject is moving across the picture and close to the camera, you will need a far higher shutter speed than if the movement is towards the camera or further from it. (Movement away from the camera similarly requires an appropriate shutter speed — but the picture is seldom of much interest.)

Fuzzy focusing can be cured by... careful focusing. There are very few subjects appropriate to article illustration where there is no time to focus carefully. If such an occasion should arise, then zone focusing can be adopted. Focus where the action is likely to occur and let the camera's *depth of field* take care of the focus.

The only other advice that can be offered in the form of a basic rule for tiro photographers is:

COMPOSE THE PICTURE

Composition is a major subject. For the article-writer taking the occasional photograph to illustrate his work, however, let me offer a few broad principles:

- Avoid having the subjects looking out of the picture — the reader will look out too.
- Try to frame the picture within itself — photograph the church through the lych-gate, or include a tree and its bough at the top and the side of a picture. Either of these devices will tend to hold the eye within the picture.
- Arrange any action so that it moves into the picture rather than — once again — drawing the eye out of the picture.
- Avoid the centre of the picture: better, arrange the subject(s) at one or more of the one-third points. (One-third of the width in from either side and one-third of the depth away from top or bottom.)

- Ensure that the foreground contains something of interest — a person admiring the view in the background, or the main subject of the picture, or even just old paving stones leading the eye on to the person working in the doorway.
- Use the camera vertically for upright pictures and horizontally for horizontal pictures.
- Take plenty of pictures and ruthlessly discard any that "don't quite look right". Professionals seldom use more than about twenty per cent of the pictures they take.

and finally,

- Keep the picture simple, the simpler the better. Note how striking and effective are the simplest-looking advertisements; emulate them. (This takes us all the way back to the first rule — decide on the subject; once that is done, your pictures can easily be kept simple.)

Remember too, when photographing in black and white, that you do not have the colour of a subject to make it stand out from the background. In black and white photography you have to rely on light and shade to provide the contrasts. The sun immediately behind the camera gives dull lighting. The sun to one side produces depth-giving shadows — except at midday, which is therefore a bad time to take photographs. And the sun in front of you, so long as you adjust the exposure to allow for it, can produce spectacular effects — but take care that the sun does not shine directly on to the lens.

Picture subjects

For your writing you need to cultivate an enquiring mind and an interest in a wide variety of subjects. Similarly, for the accompanying photography, you should cultivate a "seeing eye" — an eye for a good picture — and again, a variety of subjects.

What is this "seeing eye"? Inevitably of course, it is indefinable. It is the identification — and seizing of — the unusual, the significant, the poignant. It is what distinguishes a David Bailey from a Joe Bloggs. The seeing eye recognizes the humour in a visual situation that the man in the street passes by. (Even the most simple or puerile humour will often suffice.) It can be the noticing of the old man's raised eyebrows as the pretty girl walks by. It can as easily be the hilarious juxtaposition of two individually staid advertising phrases — or even two conflicting traffic signs.

But the "seeing eye" is also the ability to make a well-composed picture of an everyday situation. If the picture is good and the composition striking, the editor may not trim in to the subject alone. (But not all editors appreciate artistic composition.)

Given the "eye for a picture", the next requirement is to build up a stock of pictures that can accompany your articles. An article may "carry" anything up to perhaps half a dozen illustrations. Your aim therefore should be to collect, not just single photographs, but batches of pictures about each of your chosen subjects. (See Chapter 2.) Then, as you gain more photographic experience, or become more interested, collect batches of pictures of new subjects that interest you — pictorially. These sets will, in turn, lead to your reading up the subject of the illustrations. Your writing will then be to accompany the pictures rather than the reverse.

On occasions you may be able to sell a batch of pictures with little more written support than long captions (see below). Motoring, caravanning, cycling magazines and the like occasionally take such features. Writing and photography complement each other particularly well too in the general interest and "how to" article markets. Just because you think of yourself as a writer, do not overlook occasional sales of pictures alone. As already mentioned, the "Odd Snap" type of feature is often an attractive market.

Other illustrations

Although black and white photographs are the most commonly used illustrations to magazine articles, there are other possibilities. If you can obtain very old pen and ink drawings from ancient books long out of copyright, these can be very attractive illustrations to the right article. So too can similar "out of copyright" black and white prints of scenery etc. — the sort of picture produced to be framed.

If you cannot get hold of your own such ancient pictures and prints there are picture agencies — most notably the BBC Hulton Picture Library — which will provide them, for a fee. (See the *Writers' & Artists' Yearbook* for an up-to-date list of picture libraries.)

If you are at all artistic yourself, you can sometimes produce your own drawings for reproduction. This is particularly appropriate for DIY features or illustrations of patterns or *motifs*. I have illustrated the occasional article of mine with a careful black ink drawing on cartridge paper. (A brand new nylon tipped pen is ideal: line width is less readily controlled with a used pen.) Important points to watch when producing your own drawings are:

- the drawing will be reproduced smaller than you draw it: ideally therefore, make your drawing twice as big as the usual illustrations in your target magazine; (Minor blemishes in your drawing will happily be lost in the reduction process.)

- reduced-size reproduction means that lines too appear of reduced thickness, so do not use over-thin lines or include unnecessary detail;
- you need not "letter up" any drawing even where this is required: provide an annotated photocopy as a key and the editor will have a staff artist finish off your drawing. An artist's lettering will be far better than yours;
- typists' correction fluid is an ideal — and acceptable — means of correcting your line drawings.

Captions

And finally, a picture — photograph or line drawing — is of little value to anyone without a caption. (A caption is the description printed beneath almost every published picture.) Imagine a captionless picture of a street scene; no one would know where it was. It might almost be one of these "Identify the holiday location in this picture" competitions. Once you explain where it is and why it is important the picture is immensely more interesting.

To ensure that you cover everything necessary in a caption, check, wherever appropriate, against the journalists' questionnaire. Check the answers to the "5WH test":

W — Who?   — eg: Who is in the picture?
W — What?   — eg: What is the person doing? *or*
                  What is the picture of?
W — Why?   — eg: Why is the person doing whatever is being done?
W — Where? — eg: Where was the picture taken?
W — When?   — eg: When was the picture taken?
H — How?   — eg: How is the person doing whatever is being done?

Clearly, the caption for a picture of an antique would only cover *What?* But the answer to that question should itself explain *Where* it came from, *When* it was made, and perhaps *Who* made it, and *How* it was made. Think about the "5WH" questions for every caption; they will always be a useful guide, even though they are not all universally applicable.

73

7

Presentation and Salesmanship

You have now written, and polished, your article; and you have long since decided on the market to which you hope to sell it. But the article-writing business is a buyers' market. The editor may desperately need something good to fill a two-page slot but he can always fall back on a staff-written piece. As a freelance writer you have to persuade the editor to buy your wares.

Assuming that your market research (Chapter 3) has been done well, and that your article idea (Chapter 2) is a good one, you still have to present it properly. If you do not, almost irrespective of the quality of your writing, it will not sell. Presentation is an important part of article-selling.

The days when you could submit a hand-written article in an old school exercise book are long gone — if they ever existed. Your work today must be well typed. Which means you need access to a typewriter — or a typist. And I have already commended to you my own method of working — typing my work myself, amending the tangled manuscript as I type. No typist could do this work as well as I do it myself. So ... you need a typewriter.

Equipment

You don't need a word processor or an IBM golf-ball typewriter; almost any machine will do, at least when you start. If you are not an expert typist, and can afford the price, an electric typewriter has the marked advantage of making your inexpert typing look expert. (It evens out the key pressure.) Get a reconditioned second-hand office machine perhaps, or a new "semi-portable". The bigger the machine the better. But if you are strapped for cash, any working typewriter will do — manual or electric, portable or office. Just as long as it has an ordinary — *pica* or *elite* — typeface. Editors will not look kindly on work submitted in any of the more unusual typefaces — mock handwriting or large and small capitals, for instance.

Whilst thinking about equipment, let us review all that the article-writer will need. It is not a lot. You will need, as well as the typewriter:

- a two-hole filing punch — so that you can file copies of correspondence and output;
- a small ("Bambi" or similar) stapler to staple the pages of your

articles together; (All editors are haemophiliac and object to pins and paperclips.)

- some file covers — for correspondence and for copies of articles;
- some document wallets — or save any A4 envelopes that come through your letter box and use them — in which to keep cuttings, notes, etc.;
- reference books — see Appendix for recommendations.

The materials you will need are a similarly small list:

- good quality (70 gsm or better) white A4 size paper for the articles and for letters;
- thin "bank" (45 gsm) A4 size paper for carbon copies of articles and correspondence;
- carbon paper — if you use the cheapest, discard it frequently — excess economy is counter-productive;
- typewriter ribbons (single colour, black only) — I prefer the nylon ribbons as they make the typescript look sharper than do the ordinary cotton ribbons. Do not continue to use the ribbon when it is "tired"; replace it;
- typists' correction fluid and correction paper. Where would we be without it?

Typing the article

You are now ready to type your article for submission to the magazine at which it is aimed. Editors require typescripts to be in a more-or-less standard form — for good reasons, as I explain below.

The article must be typed double-spaced (that is, on alternate single-spaced lines — but your typewriter will probably have a lever to let you adjust automatically to double spacing) with wide margins. Allow margins of about 40-50 mm on the left side and at least 25 mm at top, bottom and right side. (My typewriter works at approximately ten character spaces per 20 mm — it is 12 to the inch — and I set my margin indicators for A4 paper at 20 and 83. The edges of the paper itself are at 0 and 100.) The double spaced lines allow for editorial corrections and changes to your text; the margins are used for instructions to the printers.

Insert the paper in the typewriter — a top sheet, a carbon, and a sheet of thin, bank, paper. The original is submitted to the editor but you must always keep a copy. Editors do, very occasionally, lose typescripts. Roll the paper down about 10 cm and, in capitals, type your article title — more or less centrally across the page — and underline it. Roll down a further 2 to 3 cm and type your name

Shoe money circulated widely in China throughout the nineteenth and early twentieth century. In 1925 however, the Nanking government decided to change to the international shape for their bullion bars and shoe money was no more.

You can buy your own yuan pao or tung pao coin from the T'ang dynasty today for only a couple of pounds or so. Pan liang or wu chu coins from much earlier can be had for about £10. Knife and spade coins too can sometimes be purchased – but these will cost around £50 – £70 each. Shoe money is scarce – and expensive, of course.

For just a few pounds though, you can own a Chinese bronze artefact dating from at least fifteen hundred years ago. No other piece of antique Chinese bronze can be had so readily – or so cheaply.

....   END

Gordon Wells
Layangan
████████████
███ W Sussex

CASHING IN ON CHINESE HISTORY

Gordon Wells

Maybe, like me, you have thought of coin collecting as a rather dull hobby. A bit like collecting stamps – those tiny bits of paper over which enthusiasts pore, studying watermarks and counting perforations. (This seems to be as pointless as counting the tiny perforations in those well-known tea-bags!) And certainly some coins still strike me the same way.

But not all coins are just round metal discs. There are other shapes, and some coins take us back thousands of years into ancient history. Chinese coins particularly are both steeped in history and often picturesque in appearance.

There are conflicting claims for having issued the first coinage. King Gyges of Lydia (now part of Turkey) issued oval pellets of gold-silver alloy over two thousand seven hundred

Fig. 7.1
Setting out the typescript: the first and last pages of one of my articles. (See Figure 4.1 for the start of the same article in hand-written draft.)

centrally; underline that too. Roll down again, about 3-4 cm, indent five spaces (set your tabulator to the five-space indent to ensure consistency) and begin the article.

At the end of each paragraph, miss one double-spaced line; start each new paragraph, like the opening one, five spaces in from the margin. If, following your model, you are providing headings within the article, miss one double-spaced line before and after the heading, which should be underlined. Otherwise, as already mentioned, save underlinings for words to be printed in italics.

When you start a fresh page, roll the paper down 2-3 cm. Type along the first line, well spaced out, a key word from the title, your surname, and the page number. The key word and your name should be underlined. Another form of "strap", as this is known, is to put the same details on three single-spaced lines up in the top right corner of each sheet. The strap is merely to avoid confusion should one page be misplaced in the editorial office or at the printers.

At the end of the article, roll down a couple of double-spaced lines and make a short line of full-stops in the centre, followed by END. Roll down to near the foot of the page and, at the left margin, single-spaced, type your name and address in full. Figure 7.1 shows the layout of typical first and last pages of an article typescript — one that I sold recently.

Now you need a cover page. Just as on the first page, type the title and your name about 10 and 13 cm down from the top. Roll down a further 5-6 cm and type, at the left margin, "Approximately 000 words on 0 sheets of paper." (Quote the number of words to the nearest 50 on articles under 1000 words and to the nearest 100 on longer articles and when in doubt round up.) On the next line, if appropriate, specify the number of accompanying black and white photographs.

Finally, roll down to near the foot of the page and — as on the final page — type your name and address, single spaced, at the left margin. Commonly, this cover sheet is used by editors to arrange for your payment. The cover sheet goes to the accountants; the manuscript goes to the printer — your name and address are on both.

It is my practice to provide a caption sheet for any illustrations as part of — but not a continuation of — the typescript. Like the article itself, the captions should be typed double-spaced, with letters or reference numbers to allow them to be associated with the correct pictures. The caption sheet(s) should also carry the article title and your name and address — again, for safety.

Picture presentation

Editors like illustrations accompanying articles, and they like them to be big. The preferred size always used to be 10" × 8" — but with increasing costs more editors appear willing to accept prints of a smaller size. Prints sized 8" × 6" seem acceptable anywhere (and many press releases are now that size) with 5" × 4" a minimum admitted as being acceptable. (On two or three recent occasions I have succeeded in selling articles accompanied only by enprints. These are, of course, only acceptable when the subject is big and clear in the print and the pictures are intended for only small reproduction, such as a single column width.)

As we have already discussed, it is wisest for the article-writer who takes the occasional photograph to have the processing done commercially. Order "selective enlargements" to 8" × 6" size, on glossy paper, *with bled edges* (that is, with no white borders). These not only look more professional but you get more picture for your money. Only glossy prints are acceptable for reproduction.

Editors seem to vary on where they want the captions. Some like them to be sellotaped to the back of the pictures; others specify separate caption sheets. As explained above, I usually provide a separate sheet of captions but with each caption sufficiently spaced so that the caption sheet can be cut up in the editor's office if necessary. But whether the captions are attached to the pictures or separate on a caption sheet, ensure that picture and caption can be adequately associated. And — for identification purposes — the back of every print must bear your name and address. For this, as for many similar purposes, I use tiny address labels.

Photographs are liable to damage in the post. A photograph folded in two is a photograph ruined: it cannot then be used for reproduction. Photographs accompanying articles must therefore be protected. It is convenient to protect photographic prints with a piece of card fractionally larger; an elastic band stretched diagonally across two corners will hold the package together better than a paper clip. (A paper clip may damage the prints — yet editors almost always use them.)

(Sometimes, when you are better known to an editor, you may be able to sell him photographs as contact prints. Send the contacts with the article and the editor will tell you which negatives he wants enlarged. Or he may even — if you are prepared to agree — take the negatives, have his own enlargements made, and return the negatives. All at minimal cost to you. But don't try this approach on a new editor contact, or on the editor of a small magazine. It is only worth adopting with bigger publications with their own photographic facilities, and when you yourself are well known to them.)

Despatching the article

Before actually despatching your article, make one final check that it is as good as you can make it. Use the check list at Figure 7.2.

A "just before posting" article check list

1 Is the TITLE gripping?
2 Has it a good OPENING paragraph?
3 Is it the right STYLE for the market?
4 Is it the right LENGTH for the market?
5 Is it CORRECT in every detail?
6 Is there enough MEAT in it?
7 Does it FLOW smoothly — and swiftly?
8 Have you cut out all UNNECESSARY words?
9 Does the typescript LOOK attractive — professional?
10 Would YOU buy it?

Fig. 7.2

All is now ready for you to despatch your article, plus pictures if you are offering any, to the magazine for which it was designed. There is a school of thought that says, "Just send it — any editor can see what it is and who it is from; he knows it's on spec and he knows you expect it to be paid for, or returned."

My own view is that the article should always be accompanied by a brief covering letter. That seems to be no more than polite, and normal business practice. After all, I am a salesman offering my product for sale; the editor has — usually — not asked for it; anything that I can do to help make a sale is worth doing.

But let the covering letter be little more than just a formality. The editor does not need you to tell him that the information came from such-and-such a reference book. Nor does he want you to apologize for that mass of hand-written alterations. Don't apologize; just retype it. In time, as you sell more and more features to the same magazine, you may build up a working relationship with the editor: until then, confine yourself to business. (But see below for query letters.)

My own, almost standard, letter to an editor, covering an article submitted on spec, goes like this:

Dear Mr/Mrs/Ms/Miss ...

I enclose herewith, for your consideration for publication at your normal rates, a 000 word article 'TITLE' about 'something-or-other'. (... together with 00 photographs.)

If the article is of use I would appreciate, in addition to payment, a copy of the issue of MAGAZINE in which it appears, for my records. If it is not of use I would appreciate the return of the article. I enclose the customary stamped addressed envelope.

Yours sincerely

Gordon Wells

Enc: 'TITLE' mss (plus 0 pix)
   SAE

Points to note in my letter are:

- I write to the editor or features editor by name whenever I can. The relevant names are usually found on the magazine contents page or in the *Writers' & Artists' Yearbook* — but try to ensure that you are up-to-date, by looking at a recent issue of the magazine.
- I mention what the article is about, in case the title is not self-explanatory.
- I ask for a copy of the issue containing the article. If I don't ask, I don't get. If I do ask, I still don't always get a copy — some editors tend to forget. (But some, of course, are very good about copies.)
- I enclose a stamped addressed envelope in case of rejection. The envelope is sometimes also used for an acceptance letter or for the payment cheque. Make sure that the envelope is big enough to hold the material you are despatching and is sufficiently stamped for second-class return.
- And of course, the most important point of all is that it is a letter. Do not try to deliver your article personally to the editor. Editors are very busy people, they can do without visits from tiro freelance writers, usually seeking advice. If and when an editor wants to see or speak to you, he will telephone you. (But don't sit in waiting for that call.)

Editors would undoubtedly prefer all submissions to arrive on their desks unfolded. But A4 envelopes are very expensive. And not all editors pay big money. My practice is to send longer, unillustrated, articles folded in half only and shorter ones folded twice to fit into DL sized envelopes. (DL is the size of the usual long business envelope.)

Where, for an illustrated article, I have to use a particularly large envelope, I sometimes enclose a stamped addressed label for return. This keeps the weight, and therefore the cost of postage, down, and no editor has yet complained.

Timing submissions

If your article is not tied — as, for instance, was my Hallowe'en one — to a specific publication date, then when you submit it is of little consequence. But many articles are, in one way or another, time-related. It is important therefore that they reach the editor at the right time for his consideration for the appropriate issue.

It is no use whatsoever submitting an article about Christmas cards or mistletoe customs to a monthly magazine in November. The Christmas issue will long since have gone to the printers.

So, when should you submit your time-related articles? Ignoring Christmas for the moment, you will not go far wrong if you work to the following timetable. It allows for the editorial thought-process: it does not merely indicate the last possible date before material goes to the printers:

Daily papers (including evenings)	: 2-4 weeks ahead
Weekly magazines	: 6-12 weeks ahead
Monthly magazines	: 3-6 months ahead
Quarterlies	: 6-12 months ahead

The "Bumper Christmas Issue" of any magazine is probably being planned — if only in the back of the editor's mind — all year round. July is by no means too early to send your Christmas offering to either a monthly or a weekly magazine.

Query letters

Before writing some articles it is worth investigating whether the editor of your choice — or any editor — is likely to be interested in buying it. Many American magazines virtually insist on a preliminary letter in advance of a manuscript. But this is often more a reflection on the length of article favoured by these magazines. Many British magazines use shorter articles than their American counterparts; for short features a query letter is much less appropriate.

So, when should you send a prior query to the editor? There are no hard and fast rules, but in my view an article of 1000 words or less does not justify a query letter; an article of 2000 words or more deserves prior editorial consideration; and in between ... it depends.

It depends on the amount of research and prior expense that the article entails. I have just queried an editor about an idea for an article based on a postal questionnaire survey of several well-known people's experiences and views. The circulation of the questionnaire would have put me to considerable effort and expense; the collation of the views into a feature article would have meant many hours' work. So I asked first — and got a refusal. (Before giving up the idea I shall try it out, still in prior query form, on several other suitable magazines.)

A query letter is a sales 'pitch'. You are seeking to interest the editor in your idea; to sell the idea and your ability to carry it out. If the editor writes back expressing interest in your idea you have half-sold the finished article. And on the odd occasion you might get a firm commission for it — but this is less likely until your work is already well known to the editor. (When you have sold him half-a-dozen really good articles, the editor might commission the seventh — on an idea query.)

A good query letter is therefore worth the investment of time and thought. It should tempt the editor by offering him an interesting title and an idea of the fascinating contents. To some extent, the editor will judge your ability to write from your letter — so make it a good one. Figure 7.3 is a reproduction of the letter I sent recently to *SHE* magazine; the idea interested them; I wrote the article and they accepted it. It will probably appear in print before this book does.

Sell a series

Finally, there is one thing even better than selling an article to an editor — and that is selling a whole series of articles as yet unwritten. You will not achieve this happy state with your first few published articles, but you should always keep your antennae tuned for opportunities.

When submitting a single article to a monthly "trade" magazine recently, I offered the editor the idea of a series of similar articles on kindred subjects. I had noted that the magazine had a variety of regular one-page features; I had also noted the absence of anything on "my" subject. My approach paid off. The editor liked the idea and has asked for a regular article every other month. The first few subjects are agreed, all I have to do is deliver the goods, and maintain the quality.

Think back to the ideas on professionalism that I expounded in Chapter 1. For my new series of articles I have no need for further market research or salesmanship. And I have sorted out the basic ideas already. In all, I reckon that I have "saved" about thirty to forty per cent of the normal work. And the rate of pay the editor has agreed was very good even without that "saving".

Keep your eyes open for such opportunities. After all, when you suggest such an idea, the worst that can happen is that the editor turns you down. But do work it all out carefully before you make an offer. If you fall down on a commitment the editor will not be pleased.

Gordon Wells

Layangan ▓▓▓▓▓▓▓ ▓▓▓▓ West Sussex ▓▓▓▓ ▓▓▓▓▓▓▓ ▓▓481

---

20 Aug 82

The Features Editor
SHE
National Magazine House
72 Broadwick Street
London W1V 2BP

Dear Ms Whiter

I am writing to enquire whether you might be interested in an article about the need - or otherwise - of keeping all the bits of paper that we collect in our daily lives. Do we need to keep our bank statements, and if so, for how long? Is it necessary to retain the bill for that new pair of shoes? Is there any sense in keeping gas, electricity and telephone bills after you have paid them? What would be the consequences of losing share certificates, unit trust certificates, National Savings certificates, SAYE contracts?

These, and many more questions like them, are of great importance to many people - yet many do not realise it. I think I can prepare an interesting and helpful article along these lines. Would you be interested in considering such a piece? I would of course prepare and submit it on spec.

The title of the article could perhaps be something like PAPER-KEEPING: SHOULD YOU OR SHOULDN'T YOU? I thought it might make about 1500 words but you may have other ideas. Although I would, as I say above, submit on spec, I would nevertheless appreciate some advance idea of the payment you might be able to offer for such an article if you are interested.

I enclose a stamped addressed envelope for your reply.

Yours sincerely

Gordon Wells

Gordon Wells

Enc: sae

Fig. 7.3
A typical query letter: one that I sent recently to *SHE* magazine. It was successful in that the idea and the article were accepted.

8

Business Matters

It doesn't matter that you are only writing in your spare time; from the moment that you start trying to sell your articles, you are "in business". And you need to be businesslike about it. You need to keep records of your output — and where each article is — and you will have to keep account of your expenditure and earnings.

At the same time, you are a writer, not a book-keeper. What you need is the least-time-consuming method possible of keeping records and accounts. The less time that is spent on business matters, the more time there is for writing.

I have already mentioned, in the previous chapter, one of the first aspects of being businesslike: your letters to editors. But I did not then mention the notepaper. As you sell more articles, this needs to look professional — not amateurish. You will be operating in a world where all business letters are typed, on A4 paper; and all businesses use headed notepaper. I recommend therefore that, when you are selling articles fairly frequently, you invest in a supply of headed notepaper.

Do not go in for anything too "pushy", nor anything too "twee". Leave large flamboyant headings to the local shopkeeper, and flowery script to the society ladies. Buy good quality A4 paper and have it printed with your name and address, in the simplest, plainest type. Don't say "Author" or "Freelance writer" or whatever — there should be no need. A reproduction of my own notepaper is shown at Figure 7.3.

Keeping records

Even before you invest in printed notepaper you will want to start keeping records of which article you have sent where and with what result. The system that I use — developed over the years — is, I think, as simple as is possible. Yet it records all that I need to know.

I use A4 sheets of narrow-lined paper, marked out in a series of equal-width, narrow columns. I start two fresh sheets each year. On the first sheet, the first column is merely a sequence of numbers, from 1 at the start of each year. In the second column, as I write them, I note down the keyword of each article title. In subsequent columns, alongside each title, I note each magazine to which I offer it, and the date of despatch. Rejections I don't note here — they are obvious.

	TITLE	TO/DATE → 1	2	3	4	A = Accept C = Copy P = Paid 5	6	PAID £
	1982/3							
1	Letters	FLW 8/4	Success 17/4 ▌A C //					—
2	Write On	H+C 8/4	Twinn 20/4	Lady 13/5	Ch. Her 12/6	CGA 10/7	∿∿	
3	Snake	W'end 18/4	Revue 12/5					
4	Speak up	H+C 30/4	▌A					
5	Jade	Ch Her 6/5	▌A C P					13-00
6	Take note	Living 16/5	Lnd D Post 19/7 ∿∿					
7	Freelancing	AP 20/5	▌A					
8	Writers' Spread	PLW 22/5	▌A P					4-00
9	Chin coins	Lady 28/5	H+C 6/7	Homemaker 7/8 ▌A				
10	Promoted	Surveyor 1/6	▌A					
11	Barg. Antiq	Anr. Coll 6/6	Lady 17/6	Twinn 10/7	A?			
12	Hallowe'en	Twinn 20/6	▌A C P					25-00
13	Dragons	RSPCA 1/7	Cov ET-ci 31/7					
14	Meetings	Surveyor 10/5	▌A					
15	Write	PSLG 22/8	▌A					
16	Paper keepg	SMC 30/8	▌A P					90-00
17	Animal Antiq	RSPCA 10/9	C. Life 9/x	Sig. 13/11				

TITLE	SUBMISSIONS TO	DATE	A/R	C	PAID £		
1982/3							
Letters	FLW	8/4	R		———		
Write On	H+C	8/4	R		———		
Letters	Success	17/4	Ⓐ	✓	Nil		
Snake	W'end	18/4	R		———		
Write On	Twinn	20/4	R		———		
Speak up	H+C	30/4	Ⓐ				
Jade	Ch. Herald	6/5	Ⓐ	✓	13-00		
Snake	Revue	12/5	R		———		
Write On	Lady	13/5	R		———		
Take Note	Living	16/5	R		———		
Freelancing	AP	20/5	Ⓐ				
Writers' Spd.	PLW	22/5	Ⓐ		4-00		
Chin coins	Lady	28/5	R				
Promoted	Surveyor	1/6	Ⓐ				
Bargain Antiq	Anr. Coll	6/6	R				

Fig. 8.1
My actual record sheets for articles written and submitted recently.

When an article is accepted I make a black square *blob* — just so that it stands out — in the next column and write a capital A (for accepted). When the article is published and I receive the copy that I ask for, I write C in the same column. And when I get paid, I write a P in the same column. And in the extreme right-hand column, on the relevant article line, I note the payment received.

A glance at this sheet tells me how many articles I have written to date. A quick count (of black blobs) shows how many have been accepted. My present success rate is about sixty per cent sales.

Because I like to know which decisions are outstanding — which editors have yet to respond to my offered articles — I use a second sheet of similarly ruled paper. (Examples of both sheets are shown in Figure 8.1.) But, of course, I use it differently. Across five columns are the headings: Title, To, Date, A/R & C, Paid. (The abbreviations in the fourth column are of course for accept/reject and copy received.)

Each time I despatch an article to an editor I use a new line on this sheet. (This sheet is a record of submissions whereas the first sheet was a record of articles written.) A typical entry would read: "Chinese coins", Lady, 28/5, R____. Several lines later there is a similar entry for another magazine. And several more lines later there is this entry: "Chinese coins", Homeowner, 7/8,Ⓐ.... The A is ringed to more readily attract my attention, but there is nothing else on this line yet — it has not yet been published nor have I been paid. (There is, in fact, a pencilled "20" indicating the payment, in pounds, that I anticipate. But that is merely the result of an evening spent reviewing achievements rather than writing.)

From a glance at the submissions sheet I can quickly tell how many editorial decisions are outstanding — and for how long. Sometimes I send a polite "chaser" letter; if I know an editor well I might telephone to find out what the position is; most often, I just wait.

The longer you keep records such as I have outlined above, the more you will realize three truths about editors:

- Editors seldom waste time writing letters — but sometimes, if you are lucky, they will telephone.
- Some editors dislike making decisions about submitted articles before they need to use them. (But they quickly reject all unsuitable work, so no news is usually fairly good news.)

The third "truth" is really only the second one expressed in a different way. It is, nevertheless, worth mentioning:

- Editors often hold on to work for quite a while before they use it or reject it.

(It is good business sense to make a written note of any telephone discussions with an editor. He may agree a price for your work — and then, quite inadvertently, forget what he agreed. This happened to me; I reminded the editor of our telephone agreement and got an apology closely followed by a further cheque to top up the unintended underpayment. I don't trust my memory on such matters: I always make a note.)

But with editors so loth to put pen to paper, how do you know if your work has been accepted or rejected, or just lost? The only answer, I fear, is that you will gradually get to know different editors' responses. Almost all magazines will reject unsuitable material within about a month. Many magazines will confirm acceptance, too, within about a month — but many expect the writer to interpret non-rejection as "probable acceptance for use some time in the future". It is all most unsatisfactory, but there is little any one writer can do about it. And of course, you will seldom be paid for a "retained" article until it is actually published.

Keeping accounts

Mention of payment leads us conveniently on to the need for the writer to keep accounts. The writer needs to keep financial accounts for two reasons:

- to ascertain whether or not he is making money,
- to satisfy the tax collectors (and in order to minimize his tax liability).

Your article-writing may be only a very occasional hobby; you may — unbelievably — not care whether or not you make a profit; but you should KNOW. You may be making good money from some of your writing activities, while making disastrous losses on another aspect. If you have that information you can (should) concentrate your activities on the profitable activities.

Think about the cost of writing. Stationery and postage are the major ongoing expenses and they will not vary much with different types of writing. It is your time and your research activities that vary with each article. And you are probably not costing all of those expenses.

The time and money spent on research can be considerable. It may not be a good investment. Before starting the subject research for an article, think about the economics: you can easily spend, say, £25 on research (postage, travel, photocopies, etc.) for a small feature article. If the article sells for £60 the expenditure is perhaps worth while; but supposing the article is rejected? (It happens to all of us on occasions.) If you can use the same research for several articles earning an overall £200 the research expenditure is well justified. You can seldom be precise about research costs and the like, but it is always worth thinking about costs and possible returns before starting.

Just as keeping records of submissions and acceptances is important to the writer, so too is the keeping of accounts. But again, you are a writer, not a book-keeper. So the accountancy should be minimized.

Over years of changing methods I have, I think, developed a simple yet complete system. I use a ready-ruled Accounts Book that gives me a "date" and a "details" column plus 14 "cash" columns. The first two cash columns are used simply for all receipts and all expenditure, and they allow me to see my overall profitability at a glance. The next five columns *repeat* the expenditure, under different classifications:

— postage
— research (books, magazines, photocopies and library order fees)
— stationery and pictures
— travel
— others (expenses not significant or frequent enough to warrant separate listing).

These subdivisions make it easy for me to categorize my expenditure in my annual tax return. To date, the Tax Inspector has been satisfied with the details I provide and has allowed all of my expense claims.

(As a guide for your own approach to the authorities, the Tax Inspector has accepted my claims for: telephone rental, for incoming calls; car mileage at standard rates; a small, regular, payment to my wife, for her help in research etc.; the replacement of my capital equipment, as necessary; and for expanding my filing system.)

Because I am engaged in more than one writing and associated activity, I also repeat my record of expenditure in a further series of columns. You may or may not find this useful. My own headings, merely as an example, are:

/book in hand/articles/lectures/books in print/future ideas/ general/.

Figure 8.2 shows part of one of my accounting sheets.

Date	Details		Receipt	Exp.	Post	Res ch	Stat'y & Pix	Travel
	82/3 Run Total B/F		//////// ////	//// ////				
17 Sep	Envelopes			59			59	
28 Sep	Post + order 'New Writer'			82	12	70		
	Pay L. Sep.		20 -					
1 oct	9 sets cuttings + post		9 16		16	9 -		
4 oct	Post Macmillan			12	12			
4 oct	Royalties - Griffin TE2	B	96 03					
	Pay. Cn. Herald - H2F5	A	16 -					
5 oct	Post + ort - Peach re 11/83 w/c			28	28			
8 oct	Notebook + batteries		1 49				1 49	
	Pay. Townsum. Halloween	A	25 -					
10 oct	Post + ort C. Life			33	33			
	Post + ort SWE			31	31			
	Photocopies - questionnaire			15			15	
	Post + ort. Townsum			25	25			
11 oct	Film KA64 and FP4. Leu		7 78				7 78	
13 oct	Fares to A + B			80				80
	Post + order - paper		32 16				32 16	
	Post + order - labels		2 65		15		2 50	
15 oct	Extra pay. Surveyor - Spkg.	A	20 -					
	Post + refund - Mont			28	28			
18 oct	Post . PSub			16	16			
28 Oct	Pay L. oct		20 -					

Fig. 8.2
Part of a typical page from my writing accounts book.

Other markets

Like me, many writers eventually extend their activities beyond their
initial interests. I started with photography, began writing articles to
help sell the photographs, and then soon found the writing becoming
more and more important. Then, for a while, I moved into non-
fiction book writing, leaving little time for articles or photography.
Now, I work on both books and articles at the same time, and my
photography is again playing a useful part in my activities. As a result
of one of my textbooks I have become involved in lecturing on a
training course — for which I am well paid. Some years ago I became
involved in helping to produce a publicity brochure. If it involves
writing, photography or speaking, I will have a go. And you can do
the same.

Not all writing and associated activities entail the use of the same
techniques though. Just as, in this book, you have been learning the

craft — the techniques — of article-writing, so too do other techniques have to be learnt. Writing a non-fiction book is a logical extension of a successful article-writer's activities — but the approach is very different.

Anyone seriously contemplating writing a non-fiction book is referred to my book *The Successful Author's Handbook*, Papermac, 1981. In a nutshell though, the basic differences in book-writing are:

- you sell the idea for the book to a publisher before you write much of it. (The "sales package" that you offer to a publisher consists initially of a synopsis and a brief description of objectives, market, etc. Later, to an interested publisher, you offer one or two chapters only. Only when you have a contract for the book do you write the rest.)
- you can expand yourself in a book. You are no longer searching for a thousand-word subject for a thousand-word article. It is more important to ensure that the subject is fully covered.
- you will be much more involved in the production and sales process. You will have to check proofs before the book goes to the printer. You may also be asked to assist in the selling process — including perhaps radio, or even TV, appearances.
- you will probably wait even longer for your money. Payment — other than advances — will be on a royalty basis, paid six-monthly or annually, on sales over the past period.

If you do manage to write — and sell — a book on your specialist subject, it will sometimes be worth mentioning this on your article title sheets. When writing about management communication techniques, for instance, I often note, beneath my name, "Author of *How to Communicate* (McGraw-Hill) 1978." Apart from suggesting to the editor that my article is likely to be authoritative, this note might just sell one or two more copies of my book — earning my ten per cent on each sale.

The author's scrapbook

Every writer should keep a scrapbook. When you are feeling depressed, sure that you will never be able to write another saleable word, a browse through your past successes will re-inflate your ego. But ego-trips — important though they are — are not the only justification for keeping a scrapbook.

Your scrapbook will also help to spark off ideas for new articles, for new versions of old articles, or for wholly new subjects. Your scrapbook is also one of your best reference sources. You know that you did your research properly in the first place; you can quickly pick

90

out the facts you need, and write them up again — differently — for a new feature.

Buy as large a scrapbook as possible. No matter how big it is, some of your newspaper articles will be too big to fit on to a page. Most multiple stationers sell scrapbooks — choose the one with the least garish cover. A scrapbook is money well spent.

Business questions and answers

- *Do I need an agent?*
  No. You should deal with editors yourself. Editors are accustomed to direct contact with writers. In any case, few if any agents would be prepared to take on an article-writer as a client. Agents make their living from a (normally ten per cent) commission on all of their clients' sales: individual article sales earn too little to pay for an agent's time. An agent usually only handles articles as a favour to a client whose other earnings — from books, etc. — justify his involvement.

- *What rights am I selling? (And what are "rights" anyway?)*
  Normally — unless you specify otherwise — you are offering first magazine reproduction rights when you submit an article to a magazine. Some writers mark their mss (abbreviation for manuscript) "FBSR", meaning "First British Serial Rights" but I always let this be assumed. You are saying that the article you are offering is your own work and has not already been published elsewhere. The magazine in turn is only buying the "right" to publish the article once. Should they wish to re-use it — in, for instance, an annual — they must pay for it again.

  The significance of *first* rights is that some smaller magazines are prepared to take second rights and re-use an already published article. But when you can rewrite the article to use the same facts in a different way, and thereby again sell first rights — at first rights rate of pay — second rights are largely academic. (Second rights are much more important to a writer of short stories — stories are often sold more than once.)

  When offering a once-published article, unamended, to a magazine in a foreign country you can still offer, for instance, "First American Rights" — but it is customary to point out that First British Rights have already been sold. (Major magazines on both sides of the Atlantic will, reasonably, ask for "First World Rights". Some may ask for "*All* rights" — this should be avoided whenever possible as you might want to re-use the material at a later date.)

- *Need I bother about accounts and tax matters if I only write two or three articles a year?*

  Probably not — but at the same time, you cannot claim any expenses against your writing. But whether or not you bother to keep accounts, you should declare any payment you receive for even two or three articles a year. Be assured that the Tax Inspector will know of your earnings: editors have to report all payments.

- *Can I sell articles to overseas magazines?*

  There is no reason why not — so long as you direct your submissions to appropriate publications. Market research is as important when selling overseas as it is for home sales — more so, because the cost of postage is greater. Enclose return postage for overseas magazine editors in the form of International Reply Coupons, obtainable from any Post Office. (Each IRC can be exchanged, in the overseas country, for stamps to the minimum cost of a return letter postage.) Remember though that many overseas editors expect a letter of enquiry before consideration of any article.

- *How much does article-writing pay?*

  This is a "how long is a piece of string?" question. It all depends, of course, on how much work you turn out and on which markets you sell to. A good spare-time writer might well be able to turn out at least one one-thousand-word article, or the equivalent, each week. (The constraint will often be the flow of ideas rather than the ability to get the words down on to paper.) Medium- to low-paying markets pay around £15 per thousand words. Top markets pay at least £50 (and often far more) per thousand words. An average, for the spare-time writer, might be around £25 per thousand-word article. If you can produce one article a week at that rate — and can sell perhaps fifty per cent of your production — you will earn £650 per year ... less expenses. As you gain in competence and experience you can aim your writing at higher-paying markets and increase your sales percentage. (But be careful — moving "up-market" often means fewer sales, at least initially.)

- *Should I take up article-writing as a full time occupation?*

  This too is a "piece of string" question. It depends on whether or not you like to eat well and regularly. And it depends too on your self-confidence. If you have worked your spare-time earnings up to, say, £1500 per year from about ten hours' work and if you can maintain the flow of ideas and words for, say, fifty hours a week, you may be able to earn £7500 a year. Personally, I prefer the relative security of my salaried employment plus the "jam" of my spare-time writing income. I get the best of both worlds. I have a fascinating spare-time occupation — and I eat well.